Web 1.0 – The Defir
By David Murray
Grumpy Entrepreneur"

While every precaution has been taken in the preparation of this book, the publisher assumes no responsibility for errors or omissions, or for damages resulting from the use of the information contained herein.

WEB 1.0 DOTCOM ERA DEFINED

First edition. September 25, 2023.

Copyright © 2023 David Murray-Hundley and The Grumpy Entrepreneur.

ISBN: 979-8215178225

Written by David Murray-Hundley and The Grumpy Entrepreneur.

Table of Contents

Forward 1
Introduction: From Modems to Millions 3
The Dawn of the Dotcom Era: When Netscape Ruled the Web ... 5
Venture Capital: The Silent Puppeteers of the Dotcom Era 8
Bubble Economics: A Dance of Soaring Valuations 11
Hype vs what was actually real 16
The Ecommerce Pioneers 19
The Media and Content Revolution in the Dotcom Era 24
Social beginnings 33
Unforgettable Fails of the Dotcom Era: The Cautionary Tale of Pets.com 40
Unforgettable Fails of the Dotcom Era: The Rise and Fall of TheGlobe.com 42
Unforgettable Fails of the Dotcom Era: The Rise and Fall of Go.com 44
Unforgettable Fails of the Dotcom Era: The Rise and Fall of AltaVista 46
Unforgettable Fails of the Dotcom Era: The Rise and Fall of Ask Jeeves 48
Unforgettable Chronicles of the Dotcom Era: The Tale of FuckedCompany.com 50
Business-to-Business (B2B) Dotcoms 52
The Role of Venture Capital 59
Music & Media Streaming Beginnings 65
The day the NASDAQ crashed 76
The U.S. Economy in the 1990s: A Decade of Dynamism 80
The Dotcom Delirium: A Dive into Overvaluation 82
The Interest Rate Rollercoaster: Navigating the Dotcom Era 84
Skepticism and the Dotcom Bubble: Doubt's Double-Edged Sword 86
Survivors and their Strategies 88

Y2K: The Apocalyptic Bug that Wasn't 95
Reality Distortion: The Most Outlandish Predictions of the Dotcom Era 98
Domain Drama: Tales of Squatters, Thieves, and Million-Dollar Names 101
"Ping Pong Tables and Free Snacks: The Birth of Startup Culture" 103
Lessons Learned and the Importance of Sustainable Business Models 107
The Perils of Herd Mentality During the Dotcom Era 110
The forgotten heroes of the dotcom boom 112
Legacy of the Dotcom Era and the Dawn of Web 2.0 114
Mentions/Credits 117

To everyone during the dotcom boom that had to deal with me, good and bad. Sorry to those who dealt with the bad.

To Kevin Doyle for giving me my break.

To those at Commerce One who got me on board.

And always dedicated to my girls Trina, Harriet and Georgie.

Forward

THE DOTCOM ERA FOR me, is one of those rare moments you get to be in and be part off.
So how did I end up in it, well let me tell you

1. Maybe added some things on my CV to get into an early tech company called BVR, I was 21. One of my favorite jobs I have ever had
2. That company went bust in the UK and I ended up in the company that purchased them and was in New York. So 21, I get to be part of the New York startup scene.
3. During this period I got to meet , one of my best mates Kevin Doyle who was a CTO for the business. I had other people who inspired me.
4. Then a meeting at the Piano and Pitcher in Twickenham, I got to meet Jon Sofield who, then a few weeks later Mike Hastings and John Styles, who got me into Commerce One , which is how I got to actually live the Dotcom dream or nightmare depending how you look at it.

For me it was a life of working on amazing tech, working with some amazing people and companies. It was full of living in amazing places like Monaco and the USA, driving (and sometimes crashing) Ferraris. Partying wherever I ended up, recovering with hangovers on many flights and doing crazy stuff that most people never get to do in a life time, let alone at 20-something.
The rest is history and probably something that will not happen for some time again.
It had highs, real lows and they should do a movie on it one day.

However, the Dotcom era was not the start but it probably had the biggest impact on the startup and technology world. I will forever be grateful in particular for my late father buying me a BBC Micro so that I could try and hack the Pentagon after watching War Games.

Introduction: From Modems to Millions

THE DIGITAL PULSE WE take for granted today began as a gentle hum in the not-so-distant past. Before the clamor of social media notifications and the instant gratification of high-speed downloads, there was the singular, expectant beep of the modem, signifying our nascent connection to a world just beginning to embrace the digital age.

In those initial days, personal computing was not a ubiquitous extension of our being but a novelty, often a luxury. Machines like the BBC micro, Apple II and the Commodore 64 ushered in a revolution that few could fathom would eventually culminate in the era of smartphones and omnipresent internet. This was a time when the mention of the internet would conjure images of green or amber monochrome screens, and discussions about 'surfing the web' would raise eyebrows rather than generate understanding nods.

However, for some of us, this evolution was not merely observed – it was lived. I count myself among the fortunate. My journey through the tech landscape began in the UK and took me to the pulsating heart of the US tech scene, all before the glittering dotcom boom. Indeed, I found myself woven into the fabric of this transformation, especially during my tenure at Commerce One, the dotcom prodigy. While I will touch upon that exhilarating chapter here, its tale is expansive enough to fill its own volume.

The '90s tech panorama was markedly different from today's. Conversations didn't brim with terms like "VCs", "valuations", or "IPOs". My dreams weren't of Silicon Valley stardom but of becoming a SAP engineer, having glimpsed the lucrative prospects in job classifieds.

Many of us weren't chasing the 'next big thing'; we were in tech either out of sheer love for it or the necessity of livelihood.

Stock options? I was introduced to them not out of ambition but necessity, only realizing their significance just as I was stepping into the dotcom limelight. The contrast between the UK and the US was stark. Setting foot in San Francisco, there was an electrifying buzz, a palpable tech fervor. Just a simple coffee run to a Starbucks in Walnut Creek, California, would reveal the extent of tech's permeation: almost everyone had, in some capacity, brushed shoulders with the burgeoning tech industry.

This book hopes to guide you through the tumultuous, transformative, and often untold stories of the dotcom era – a period that set the groundwork for our current digital epoch. Join me as we journey through a time of innocence, innovation, dreams, and, for some, unparalleled riches.

The Dawn of the Dotcom Era: When Netscape Ruled the Web

IN THE EARLY STAGES of the internet's development, many facets of what we now take for granted were still taking shape. The dotcom era was not just a period of booming businesses; it was the time when the foundational pillars of the internet as we know it were being established. One can hardly imagine the current web landscape without recalling the influence of the pioneers from those formative years.

Looking back to the 1990s, the web browsers that dominated my screen and those of countless others bore names that may sound archaic to today's generation. Initially, there was CompuServe, a gateway to a then-unfamiliar digital realm. But its dominance was soon eclipsed by another name, a name that became synonymous with internet browsing: Netscape.

Netscape wasn't just another browser; it was the browser. Its presence was so ubiquitous that when you thought of the internet, you inevitably thought of Netscape. As people today ensure compatibility with giants like Google or Microsoft, back then, the digital compass pointed unwaveringly towards Netscape.

Founded by Jim Clark and helmed by the youthful Marc Andreessen, Netscape Navigator took the world by storm. The browser was intuitive, user-friendly, and introduced millions to the wonders of the World Wide Web. Its IPO in 1995 was groundbreaking, both in its financial success and in signaling the immense potential of internet companies. But while Netscape soared high, it also became the prime target in the brewing browser wars.

Though Netscape was the titan of the mid-90s, Microsoft's Internet Explorer (IE) was gearing up in the background. Microsoft, with its unparalleled resources and Windows operating system's dominance, strategically integrated IE. As a result, Internet Explorer started gaining traction, initiating a fierce competition that Netscape, despite its earlier dominance, struggled to maintain against.

As the years progressed, Microsoft's aggressive tactics and Netscape's own missteps saw the latter's market share dwindling. By the end of the 90s, the browser that once introduced the world to the web had been dethroned. While Netscape's code lived on, giving birth to Mozilla Firefox, the brand itself faded.

Netscape's meteoric rise and eventual decline are emblematic of the dotcom era's volatility, setting the stage for future battles in the tech frontier.

Note -(IPO) in August 1995, Netscape had a market capitalization of over $2 billion. At the time that was a mega amount for a young company.

As the World Wide Web unfurled its vast potential, few entities stood as tall and influential as AOL and Yahoo. These giants, while now often overshadowed by the contemporary dominance of other tech mammoths, once dictated the rhythms of the internet.

America Online, or AOL, was for many the gateway to the internet. With its ubiquitous "You've Got Mail" alert, it became a household name, personifying the early days of internet connectivity. AOL offered more than just an internet connection; it was a comprehensive online service providing everything from chat rooms to news, casting a wide net that encapsulated a burgeoning online community.

Then, in the colorful tapestry of the digital age, there was Yahoo. Before the verb "to Google" became synonymous with online searching, there was another name that echoed in the corridors of the internet. Yahoo was not just another search engine; it was the search engine. If one were to reminisce about those times, the memory of the iconic Yahoo homepage, with its directory-style listing, might flood back. Whether I wanted to check the stock price of Commerce One or get the latest updates on corporations, Yahoo was my go-to. The verb "to Google" had yet to implant itself into the lexicon; instead, we "Yahoo-ed" our queries.

But like all great empires, the reigns of AOL and Yahoo weren't without their challenges. AOL's merger with Time Warner in 2000, touted as a formidable fusion of old and new media, ultimately became a textbook example of merger missteps. As broadband became prevalent, AOL's dial-up model started to feel antiquated, and its grip on the internet access market weakened.

Yahoo's trajectory, too, faced turbulence. Despite its early dominance in search and web services, Yahoo missed out on pivotal opportunities to acquire emerging giants like Google and Facebook. Over time, competition stiffened, and Yahoo's position began to waver. The strategic missteps, coupled with management turnovers, left Yahoo battling to reclaim its former glory.

While today's digital landscape is vastly different, with new titans like Google and Facebook leading the charge, the stories of AOL and Yahoo serve as vital chapters in the annals of the internet's history. They remind us of a time when the digital world was still finding its footing and underscore the transient nature of tech dominance.

Note - The merger with Time Warner and AOL in January 2000, AOL's market capitalization was approximately $222 billion however the bubble went and valuation was a lot lower.

Note 2 - In January 2000, at the peak of the dotcom bubble, Yahoo!'s market cap reached around $125 billion. You have to kind of wonder what Netscape would have been worth if it had IPOd later.

Venture Capital: The Silent Puppeteers of the Dotcom Era

AS THE DAWN OF THE dotcom era illuminated a brave new world of innovation, there was an intricate web of financial scaffolding underpinning this digital revolution: the realm of venture capital (VC). Though they often stayed behind the curtains, VCs were the driving force, enabling the birth and explosive growth of many iconic companies we associate with the turn of the millennium.

For those immersed in the tech world during the 1990s, it's almost comical to think how little the term 'VC' resonated. I'll admit, for the better part of that decade, the acronym was alien to me, and I wasn't alone in that naiveté. The dotcom landscape was a pioneering frontier where many were more preoccupied with innovation and pushing boundaries than with the financial mechanisms propelling them forward. We didn't bandy about with phrases like "angel investors" or "seed rounds." Instead, investors were just that: individuals or consortiums with deep pockets, ready to bankroll our dreams. They didn't come with halos or wings; they came with checkbooks and expectations.

The shift from a tech-centric view to one that acknowledged the strategic might of VCs was gradual for many, myself included. I remember the first time I encountered a venture capitalist. It was during a project in New York. Rumor had it that I was meeting someone influential, a bigwig who could make or break our ambitions. And yet, when the meeting transpired, I sat there, perhaps embarrassingly, without a hint of recognition. This person, who was accustomed to deference and gravitas, was, in my eyes, just another stakeholder.

But as the 90s gave way to the 2000s, the veil was lifted. Venture capitalists emerged not just as faceless financiers but as strategic partners, offering more than money. They brought networks, mentorship, and invaluable guidance, often acting as a startup's North Star. Firms like Sequoia Capital, Kleiner Perkins, and Benchmark became household names in tech circles, wielding influence comparable to the dotcoms they funded.

In retrospect, the ascent of VCs was inevitable. The dotcom era wasn't just about ideas; it was about scaling them, commercializing them, and embedding them into the socio-economic fabric. While engineers and developers were the heart and soul of the dotcom movement, venture capitalists were its lifeblood. They took nascent ideas, often jotted on napkins in cafés, and transformed them into global phenomena. And even if many of us didn't realize their impact at the time, the dotcom legacy owes as much to the boardrooms of Sand Hill Road as it does to the garages of Silicon Valley.

And this chapter wouldn't be complete without some VC stories in the dawn on the dotcom.

Mike Markkula and Apple: While not strictly a dotcom story, it's foundational for understanding the tech and VC relationship. After Steve Jobs and Steve Wozniak created the Apple I computer, they needed funds to expand. Mike Markkula, a semi-retired Intel marketing executive, was introduced to them. He wrote a business plan, invested $250,000 of his own money, and secured a line of credit for them. This early investment and Markkula's business acumen helped transform Apple from a garage startup to a major tech company.

> Sequoia Capital and Yahoo!: Sequoia Capital, a legendary venture capital firm, invested in Yahoo! during its nascent stage. Jerry Yang and David Filo had created a directory of their favorite websites called "Jerry and David's Guide to the World Wide Web". Seeing its potential, Sequoia invested in

the startup, which was later renamed Yahoo! The company went on to become one of the primary gateways to the internet during the dotcom era.

Benchmark Capital and eBay: In 1997, Benchmark Capital invested $6.7 million in a fledgling startup known as eBay. At that time, eBay was just a small online auction site. This investment is notable because of the extraordinary return it delivered. Within a year, eBay went public, and Benchmark's stake ballooned in value, representing one of the most successful VC investments of the era.

John Doerr, Kleiner Perkins, and Amazon: John Doerr of Kleiner Perkins Caulfield & Byers, another leading VC firm, famously invested in Amazon in 1995. While Amazon at that time was just a small online bookseller, Doerr's backing helped the company scale and diversify. Today, Amazon stands as one of the world's most valuable companies.

The Netscape Moment: Netscape's 1995 IPO wasn't just a success for the company, but also for the VCs who backed it. The company's public offering set off a gold rush mentality, where VCs were on the lookout for the next big internet startup. This pivotal moment effectively kicked off the dotcom boom, as investments in internet companies surged.

Bubble Economics: A Dance of Soaring Valuations

IN THE LEXICON OF MODERN startups, the term 'valuation' holds an almost mythical reverence. Founders today can be engrossed, if not consumed, by the monetary worth attached to their ventures. But to grasp the sheer audacity of startup valuations, one need only look back to the feverish days of the dotcom era.

During those heady times, valuation figures seemed to detach themselves from the gravitational pull of traditional economics. Revenue, profitability, and sometimes even a clear business model were no longer prerequisites for a sky-high valuation. The optimism surrounding the potential of the internet led investors to pump vast sums into startups, hoping to bet on the next digital gold mine. This frenzy transformed stock markets into casinos, where staggering amounts of money changed hands based on little more than hope and hype.

A case in point is Commerce One. Its journey to the stock market culminated in a July 1999 IPO, a day still etched vividly in my memory. To fathom the scale of the dotcom bubble, consider this: At its zenith, Commerce One boasted a market capitalization of a staggering $22 billion. What's even more astonishing is that, to my recollection, the firm had only managed to turn a profit in a single quarter. Such was the nature of the era: a startup's promise and potential, rather than its balance sheet, became the basis of its worth.

But as history teaches us, when financial optimism isn't anchored in fundamentals, the bubble inevitably bursts. And when it did, post dotcom crash, many behemoths with sky-high valuations vanished, while a few adaptable ones rebuilt on firmer foundations.

Reflecting on those times, it's evident that while valuations can be indicative of a company's perceived potential, they should also be grounded in reality. As the digital age continues to evolve, the lessons from the dotcom era serve as a poignant reminder: that true value doesn't come from fleeting market sentiments, but from building lasting, sustainable businesses.

But again lets talk about some of the companies that were part of this crazy time.

Pets.com: This online pet supply retailer became one of the poster children for dotcom excess. At its peak, Pets.com raised $82.5 million in an IPO, reaching a valuation in the hundreds of millions. Despite its famous sock puppet mascot and aggressive marketing campaigns, the company had a short lifespan and folded in November 2000, just nine months after its IPO.

Webvan: Another iconic symbol of the dotcom bubble, Webvan aimed to revolutionize grocery shopping with its online delivery service. The company raised over $800 million in funding and had an IPO that valued it at nearly $5 billion. Unfortunately, aggressive expansion and a flawed business model led to its downfall in 2001.

Kozmo.com: A pioneer in the promise of one-hour delivery for a range of products, Kozmo raised more than $250 million in capital. The company was prepping for a significant IPO when the bubble burst, causing it to eventually shut down in 2001 without ever going public.

boo.com: This fashion retailer aimed to merge stylish clothing with cutting-edge tech. After raising around $135 million, the company quickly burned through its capital due to a combination of technological challenges, logistical issues, and lavish spending. It folded in 2000, after only six months of operation.

Broadcast.com: Founded by Mark Cuban and Todd Wagner, Broadcast.com was an internet radio company that Yahoo! acquired for $5.7 billion in stock. While the acquisition made Cuban and Wagner billionaires, Yahoo! struggled to capitalize on the purchase, and much of the technology and services of Broadcast.com faded away in subsequent years.

Netscape: As previously mentioned, Netscape's 1995 IPO can be seen as the spark that ignited the dotcom boom. Its shares were initially priced at $28, but by the end of the first trading day, they had soared to $75, giving the company a valuation of nearly $3 billion. While Netscape had a genuine product and user base, its valuation was a sign of the fevered market of the time.

AOL's Acquisition of Time Warner: In what became one of the most infamous deals of the dotcom era, AOL, leveraging its inflated stock price, acquired Time Warner in 2000 for a whopping $165 billion. The merger, heralded as the perfect blend of new and old media, faced numerous challenges and is often cited as one of the least successful mega-mergers in corporate history.

One of my favorites back then, that actually in a afternoon paid for a Ferrari for me, was Headquartered in the heartland of America in Chicago, PurchasePro sought to capitalize on the burgeoning B2B (business-to-business) e-commerce trend. Founded by Charles E. "Junior" Johnson, the company aimed to simplify procurement processes for businesses by providing an online marketplace where suppliers and buyers could connect and transact.

The Rise: By the close of the 1990s, PurchasePro's ambitions seemed well within reach. The company's IPO in September 1999 was a resounding success, with shares opening at $7 and soaring to over $200 by early 2000. This stellar performance was reflective of the period's appetite for anything e-commerce related, and PurchasePro's business model appeared to be a surefire winner in the age of the internet.

High Profile Partnerships: Further buoying its prospects, PurchasePro entered into high-profile partnerships. One of the most notable was with AOL. This collaboration aimed to develop a B2B e-commerce platform for AOL's business clients, infusing both companies with even more credibility in the market.

The rumors circulated that PurchasePro had not even built any software, never did understand if that was true or not, but the fact they had

By 2001, the company's revenues were under suspicion. Accusations of accounting irregularities and inflated sales figures began to surface. These financial discrepancies led to investigations by both the Securities and Exchange Commission (SEC) and the Department of Justice.

PurchasePro's stock price, once a symbol of its rapid ascendancy, plummeted. The fallout from these investigations coupled with the broader collapse of the dotcom bubble culminated in the company filing for bankruptcy in 2002.

Not sure I should be thankful or not to PurchasePro but it was a ticker that I use to track on a constant basis.

They were not the only ones how ever to play the numbers, then there was Infospace.

Founded by Naveen Jain in 1996, InfoSpace aimed to provide content and services for emerging internet portals and mobile devices.

Initially, the company specialized in white pages, yellow pages, and web directories. Its positioning at the intersection of the mobile and internet sectors made it exceptionally promising, leading to partnerships with leading phone and internet service providers.

By 2000, InfoSpace's stock had surged, and at its peak, the company's market capitalization exceeded $30 billion. They boldly proclaimed their goal of becoming "the next Microsoft" and expanded aggressively through a series of acquisitions, each adding more content and services to its portfolio.

Questionable Accounting and Business Practices: The first cracks in the facade became evident when doubts about InfoSpace's revenue recognition practices surfaced. The company was accused of using a complex web of internal deals to inflate its revenues artificially. Essentially, InfoSpace was engaging in "round-trip" transactions. For instance, it would "sell" content to a company and then "buy" advertising from the same company, often at similar amounts, making it appear as though both companies were generating significant revenues from these transactions. This allowed InfoSpace to report impressive growth figures, further fueling its stock's ascent.

There were also claims that some of InfoSpace's acquisitions were less about genuine strategic fit and more about artificially boosting the company's revenues. These acquisitions were often followed by immediate write-offs of a significant portion of the acquisition cost, indicating that the assets might have been significantly overvalued during the purchase.

The Downfall: When the dotcom bubble burst, companies with questionable accounting practices, like InfoSpace, were hit hard. Skeptical investors and regulators began to dig deeper into the reported figures, leading to a loss of confidence. By 2002, InfoSpace's stock had collapsed to a mere fraction of its peak value. This rapid descent was further accelerated by a series of lawsuits and regulatory investigations.

Then this brings us to Hype and Media Hype..

Hype vs what was actually real

THE DOTCOM ERA WAS a time of unparalleled exuberance. Amid the whirlwind of tech advances and the golden promise of the internet's boundless potential, there existed a chasm between the facades many companies presented and the realities they faced. This discrepancy became especially pronounced in the strategies employed by companies to bolster their stock prices post-IPO.

Let's journey back to those frenetic days. Imagine a company freshly out of its IPO. In the scramble to maintain momentum and investor interest, it wasn't just about showcasing solid business fundamentals; it was equally about mastering the art of optics. Announcements were the order of the day. Whether it was forging a partnership with tech titans like Microsoft or Compaq, onboarding an industry-renowned executive, or even just striking a deal with the local business around the corner, any news was good news. In essence, if it could create a buzz, it was deemed worthy of a press release.

I often reminisce about my time at Commerce One, where the race for announcements felt like a high-stakes game of one-upmanship. Ariba, which later merged with SAP, and Oracle were our formidable adversaries. With news feeds from outlets like Reuters flooding Yahoo, it became a thrilling daily spectacle sat in Chiswick or Walnut Creek to see which among us had unveiled the most groundbreaking news. And the catch? This wasn't a monthly or even a weekly race. It was a day-to-day, sometimes hour-to-hour contest. The reward? A favorable bump in stock price driven by the day's narrative.

This incessant chase for headlines, however, had its pitfalls. While it propelled stock prices and drove investor enthusiasm in the short term, it often veiled the underlying health of the business. Announcing

WEB 1.0 DOTCOM ERA DEFINED 17

non-paying clients as victories or amplifying inconsequential partnerships became symptomatic of a larger issue: the blurring lines between genuine progress and mere posturing.

The list is endless about the hype marketing machine, below I talk about a few examples but could write a book on the number of PR stunts, hype machine things to happen during that era.

> Flooz: This was an attempt to create a new kind of digital currency for online transactions(sound familiar?) . Backed by significant advertising campaigns, including endorsements by Whoopi Goldberg, it couldn't gain enough traction and went under.
>
> Pixelon: Claimed to have revolutionary technology for streaming high-quality video. The company threw a $16 million launch party with top-tier artists. But it turned out their technology wasn't as revolutionary as claimed, and the founder had a questionable past.
>
> Pseudo.com: Aimed to be a major player in the internet broadcasting sphere. While it got attention for its shows and drew interests from celebrities, it burned through its cash with high production costs and couldn't generate enough ad revenue.
>
> eToys: This online toy retailer had a successful IPO and was even, at one point, valued more than Toys "R" Us. But post-holiday season sales drop, distribution issues, and competition led to its bankruptcy.
>
> Startups backed by celebrities: The dotcom era also saw many celebrities backing startups. Examples include "Shaq.com" backed by Shaquille O'Neal and

"Fashionmall.com" endorsed by supermodel Claudia Schiffer. Many of these ventures, despite the star power, didn't have sustainable business models.

Countless other e-commerce platforms: The dotcom bubble saw a proliferation of e-commerce platforms, each claiming a niche (selling furniture, cosmetics, electronics, etc.). Many of them had huge advertising budgets but couldn't figure out the logistics, supply chain, or how to turn a profit. Now doesn't that also sound familiar about 2023?

The Ecommerce Pioneers

TODAY, ECOMMERCE IS second nature to most of us. But wind back the clock, and it was an entirely different scene. Can you imagine a time when online shopping was more of a novelty than a necessity? Nowadays, if our Amazon Prime delivery takes just a day longer, we're up in arms. This brings to mind a memory from 1998. I was with Reuters back then, often finding myself visiting grand mansions on London's outskirts, homes of the uber-wealthy. On one such visit, I was ushered in through grand gates, escorted by a young lad whose father managed the vast estate. Over time, we got chatty, and he mentioned he was about to join a 'book-selling' company called Amazon. If you'd told me then what Amazon would become today, I'd have probably chuckled in disbelief. I can only hope he snagged some stock during his stint there.

So Amazon,

Amazon: From Online Bookstore to Dotcom Dominance

GENESIS (1994-1997): In the mid-1990s, the internet was still a burgeoning phenomenon, ripe with potential but largely uncharted. It was in this climate that Jeff Bezos, a former hedge fund manager, launched Amazon in 1994. Initially operating out of his garage in Seattle, Bezos envisioned a digital marketplace that started with books but would eventually encompass every conceivable product.

Why books? Bezos recognized that the vast number of book titles made it impractical for physical stores to stock them all. An online model could provide a virtually limitless inventory. In July 1995, Amazon.com went live as "Earth's Biggest Bookstore," boasting over a million titles.

Rapid Expansion (1997-1999): By 1997, Amazon had its Initial Public Offering (IPO), signaling its ambition. The stock debuted at $18 per share, setting the stage for what would become one of the most remarkable growth stories in corporate history.

But Amazon wasn't content being just a bookstore. Within a few years, the platform began to diversify, adding music CDs and movies to its inventory. The website also introduced features like customer reviews, which, while standard today, were revolutionary at the time.

By the end of the '90s, Amazon had expanded into consumer electronics, video games, software, and toys, evolving from an online bookstore into a diversified e-commerce platform. They were rapidly cementing their reputation not just for variety but also for customer service and convenience. The company introduced the 1-Click feature, which allowed repeat customers to make purchases with a single click, streamlining the online shopping experience.

Funding and Financial Challenges (2000-2002): Despite its impressive growth, Amazon was burning through cash quickly. Expansion required capital. Massive warehouses were built, software systems developed, and partnerships forged. By 2000, while the dotcom bubble was approaching its zenith, Amazon was facing financial pressures.

In the wake of the dotcom crash, many e-commerce startups vanished. Amazon survived, but not unscathed. They laid off 15% of their workforce in 2001. The stock price, which had soared to dizzying heights, plummeted from a split-adjusted high of nearly $100 per share in late 1999 to below $10 by 2001.

However, this challenging period was also a time of introspection and recalibration for the company. Amazon focused on its core strengths and began inching towards profitability. In 2001, it reported its first ever quarterly profit, albeit a modest one.

Building a Tech and Distribution Moat (2002-2005): Amazon's resilience in the early 2000s wasn't just due to its e-commerce operations. The company was also quietly laying the groundwork for what would become a dominant force in technology: Amazon Web Services (AWS). Launched in 2002, AWS represented Bezos' vision of Amazon as a technology-driven company, not just a retailer.

Moreover, understanding that quick and reliable delivery was key to e-commerce success, Amazon began investing heavily in its logistics network. Fulfillment centers sprouted across the U.S., paving the way for services like Amazon Prime, which would debut in 2005, offering two-day shipping and setting a new industry standard.

A Vision Realized: Looking back at Amazon's trajectory during the late '90s and early 2000s, it's clear that the company's success wasn't just due to its ability to capitalize on the e-commerce wave. Strategic decision-making, customer-centric innovation, and an ability to adapt quickly played pivotal roles.

While many of its contemporaries from the dotcom era faded into obscurity or went bust, Amazon emerged stronger, learning from its mistakes and consistently setting its sights on long-term goals. From an online bookstore to an e-commerce juggernaut, Amazon's journey through the late '90s and into the dotcom era is a testament to visionary leadership, resilience, and an unyielding focus on customer satisfaction.

And to think now, he takes a rocket up to space! Crazy stuff.

eBay always caught my eye, especially during my trips to the US. Something about its logo and color scheme made it stand out to me back then. Even though it made its UK debut in 1999, I didn't really dive into it until around 2002 or 2003. Whether you're a fan or not, you've got to admit: the platform has endured, still standing strong today.

eBay: The Auction House of the Internet Era

Beginnings (1995-1998): In the midst of the 1990s' technological boom, a unique online platform emerged: eBay. Founded by Pierre Omidyar in 1995, it began as "AuctionWeb," a side project in which Omidyar sought to create a digital marketplace for the sale of goods and services. The first item sold? A broken laser pointer. This seemingly innocuous sale laid the foundation for what would become a global e-commerce phenomenon.

Unlike traditional retail platforms, eBay provided an online space where individuals could auction items to the highest bidder. The concept was revolutionary; it democratized buying and selling, enabling virtually anyone with internet access to participate.

Rapid Growth and Going Public (1998-2000): By 1998, with the addition of Meg Whitman as CEO, the company was rebranded as eBay and went public. The IPO was a resounding success, reflecting the enthusiasm for dotcom businesses and the unique value proposition eBay offered. As the user base grew exponentially, eBay began to expand beyond auctions, introducing the "Buy It Now" feature, which allowed users to bypass bidding wars and purchase items immediately.

The late '90s saw eBay becoming not just a place for individuals to sell unwanted items but a legitimate platform for businesses and entrepreneurial individuals to reach a global customer base. From collectibles to cars, almost anything could be found on eBay.

Challenges and Adaptation (2001-2005): While eBay's growth was impressive, it wasn't without challenges. As the platform grew, issues like fraudulent listings, counterfeit items, and disputes between buyers and sellers began to arise. Recognizing the importance of trust in its business model, eBay introduced a feedback system, allowing buyers and sellers to rate their experiences with one another. This system, though simple, became one of the platform's defining features, fostering a community-driven approach to e-commerce.

Furthermore, to diversify its offerings and bolster its e-commerce dominance, eBay made several acquisitions during this period. The most notable of these was the purchase of PayPal in 2002, which provided eBay users with a seamless and trusted payment system.

Becoming a Global Marketplace: As the early 2000s rolled on, eBay's global presence solidified. They expanded internationally, launching dedicated sites for various countries, including the UK in 1999. The platform adapted to local cultures and tastes, ensuring a more personalized shopping experience for users worldwide.

Today, eBay remains a testament to the potential of the internet to transform how we buy, sell, and connect. Things we take for granted in many ways.

The Media and Content Revolution in the Dotcom Era

IN THE MIDST OF THE dotcom boom, while many of us were laser-focused on the tantalizing prospects of B2B and e-commerce, another transformation was quietly unfolding: the revolution in media and content. Admittedly, with my eyes set firmly on the B2B horizon, I sometimes overlooked the burgeoning media landscape. It wasn't that I was unaware; perhaps, like many, I simply took it for granted.

Cast your mind back to 1997. At Dione Internet, our ambitions were sky-high. We were on the cutting edge, attempting to pave the way for what we believed was the future: smart card readers and internet TV set-top boxes. With the enthusiasm of pioneers, we envisioned a world where these devices would be household staples, seamlessly integrating the digital world into our daily lives. Looking back, it's clear that our ideas weren't off the mark. We were simply ahead of our time.

The dotcom era was more than just websites and online shopping. It was the dawn of digital media, where content began its shift from traditional formats to online platforms. Companies started exploring ways to deliver news, entertainment, and education via the internet. Video streaming, though in its infancy, promised a future where one could watch anything, anytime, anywhere. Digital music platforms hinted at the end of the physical CD era, offering songs and albums at the click of a button.

But, like our endeavors at Dione Internet, not every early venture in the media space would find immediate success. The technology and infrastructure were still evolving, and consumer habits needed time to adjust. Yet, these initial steps were crucial. They laid the groundwork for the digital media landscape we know today—a world of streaming services, podcasts, and online journalism.

In retrospect, it's fascinating to realize how much of the media and content revolution was happening right under our noses. While some of us were engrossed in the B2B sphere or other niches, the way we consumed content was beginning its seismic shift. It's a testament to the dotcom era's multifaceted nature: a time of rapid change, boundless ambition, and a vision that often outpaced reality.

Just cast your mind to all the content you look at daily, well below is some of those pioneers that took those early steps.

Salon and Slate: Pioneering the Digital Magazine Landscape

THE DOTCOM ERA, RIFE with innovation and audacious ideas, saw the rise of many digital ventures. Among them, the ascent of online magazines—specifically, Salon and Slate—stands out. These pioneers dared to venture where traditional print journalism was hesitant, redefining how readers accessed and consumed content.

Salon: A Beacon of Independent Journalism

Genesis (1995): Salon, founded in 1995 by David Talbot, emerged from San Francisco, the hub of tech innovation. Conceived as a digital alternative to print magazines, Salon was more than just a publication; it represented a fresh perspective, blending bold political commentary with culture, art, and books.

Early Days and Vision: Unlike many startups from the dotcom bubble, Salon wasn't just about profit. Its founders saw the internet as a democratizing force for journalism—a space free from the influence of giant media conglomerates. Initial pieces ranged from insightful political critiques to daring exposes, proving that digital journalism could rival, if not surpass, its print counterpart in depth and quality.

Challenges and Evolution: Yet, pioneering a new medium wasn't without its trials. Monetizing digital content, especially in an era where readers expected online content to be free, was an uphill battle. Salon experimented with various models, from subscription services to ad-supported content. Through resilience and adaptability, it managed not just to survive but thrive, becoming synonymous with independent, incisive journalism.

Slate: The Digital Challenger with Traditional Roots

Origins (1996): Just a year after Salon's debut, 1996 saw the birth of Slate, backed by none other than Microsoft. Michael Kinsley, a seasoned journalist, was at the helm, ensuring that while the platform

WEB 1.0 DOTCOM ERA DEFINED 27

was digital, the commitment to journalistic integrity and depth was unwavering.

Balancing Act: Being bankrolled by a tech behemoth presented both advantages and challenges. While financial support wasn't a pressing concern, maintaining an independent voice was crucial. Slate aimed to strike a balance, leveraging its tech lineage to innovate in content delivery while ensuring the journalism remained uncompromised.

Innovations and Impact: Slate introduced readers to novel formats, like interactive articles and podcasts (notably "Slate's Political Gabfest"), many of which are mainstream today. It wasn't just content; it was content adapted for the digital age, interactive and dynamic.

The Broader Impact:

Redefining Journalism: Both Salon and Slate played pivotal roles in reshaping perceptions about digital journalism. They demonstrated that the digital medium wasn't just for brief news snippets; long-form, deeply researched articles had a home online. Their commitment to quality over clickbait laid the groundwork for the next generation of digital journalists and publications.

Monetization and the Digital Model: Their explorations into monetization—be it subscriptions, paywalls, or ad-supported models—provided valuable insights for the media industry. They were among the first to grapple with the challenge of making quality journalism sustainable in a digital world, a quest that remains ongoing.

Setting the Stage: The success of Salon and Slate signaled to other print publications that the digital realm was viable. Legacy publications, witnessing the potential of online journalism, began their foray into the digital landscape, leading to the diverse, multi-platform media ecosystem we see today.

In retrospect, the dotcom era was more than just a tech revolution; it was a renaissance of ideas, a period where boundaries of traditional industries were pushed. Salon and Slate, with their audacious belief in the potential of online journalism, stand as testaments to the era's spirit of innovation. They didn't just mirror the print world online; they reimagined journalism for the digital age, setting the standard for future generations of media.

The Dawn of Set-Top Boxes: From 1990s Vision to Today's Reality

BACK IN THE LATTER half of the 1990s, we were already envisioning a world where televisions would seamlessly integrate with the internet. The concept might seem a bit quaint now, given our high-tech environment, but back then, it was nothing short of revolutionary. The notion of set-top boxes, devices specifically designed to enable TVs to access the web, felt simultaneously retro and futuristic. The moniker "set-top box" itself seemed to harken back to earlier eras, even while the technology it represented was pushing boundaries.

Fast-forward to today, and our digital consumption habits have evolved in ways we could only have dreamt of in those earlier days. Now, instead of just passively watching content, platforms like YouTube have democratized content creation. For instance, I personally have ventured into this space, curating a channel called "The Grumpy Entrepreneur Startup, Scaleup Show." Admittedly, it might not rival big production houses, but it embodies the spirit of our digital age — where anyone can be a content creator.

Speaking of YouTube, it's fascinating how our viewing habits have changed. Whether you're indulging in high-octane F1 races, engrossed in dramas like Emmerdale, or like me, have a penchant for automobile-related content, there's no shortage of niche interests catered to.

But let's rewind a bit and delve into one of the early precursors to today's Smart TVs: WebTV.

WebTV: Pioneering Internet on Television

The Vision: WebTV Networks, founded in the mid-1990s, was among the first to recognize the potential synergy between the internet and television. Their promise was groundbreaking: granting TV viewers direct access to the vast world of the internet, all from the comfort of their living rooms.

The Reality: The actual experience of WebTV was both intriguing and challenging. The interface aimed to be user-friendly, and for many households, it provided their first taste of the internet. Yet, like many innovations of its time, it was ahead of its time. Navigating websites designed for computer screens on a TV presented its own set of hurdles. But more than the technical challenges, WebTV was battling against entrenched viewing habits. The idea of blending active web browsing with passive TV watching was novel and took some getting used to.

Legacy of WebTV: Although WebTV faced its share of challenges and eventually became overshadowed by emerging technologies, its importance in the annals of tech history cannot be understated. It laid the groundwork for future innovations, showing that the internet and television could, in fact, be harmoniously integrated.

As we sit today, effortlessly toggling between apps on our Smart TVs or casting content from our phones, it's worth pausing to reflect on these early ventures. The set-top boxes and initiatives like WebTV paved the way for the multimedia experience we take for granted now, reminding us that every great innovation often stands on the shoulders of earlier attempts.

So while I was writing this I did some research on some of the pioneers at the time. As I said maybe I was not paying that mich attention but was surprised how many there were at that time.

WebTV Networks (later MSN TV)

- Steve Perlman, Phil Goldman, and Bruce Leak: As mentioned, these co-founders of WebTV aimed to make the internet accessible to everyone through televisions.

Microsoft

- Bill Gates: While Gates didn't directly invent WebTV, Microsoft's acquisition and subsequent integration of the technology into its product line was significant. Under his leadership, Microsoft saw the potential of the internet-on-TV idea and sought to capitalize on it.

Sony

- Sony Internet Terminal: Sony, ever the innovator in electronics, jumped into the fray with devices like the Sony Internet Terminal, which used WebTV's service.

Philips

- Known for their consumer electronics, Philips also collaborated with WebTV to bring internet to TV screens.

Netscape

- Marc Andreessen and Jim Clark: While Netscape is more famous for its pioneering web browser, they too were considering ways to broaden internet access, which included TVs.

AOL TV

- Steve Case: As CEO of AOL, Case saw the company venture into the realm of internet-on-TV with AOL TV. This was an endeavor to merge AOL's content and services with the television experience.

Apple

- Steve Jobs: Apple, under Jobs, introduced the Apple Interactive Television Box in the mid-90s as a precursor to later developments like Apple TV. While this early venture didn't go commercial, it showed Apple's interest in the space.

Intel

- Intel Intercast: In the mid-90s, Intel introduced technology that allowed broadcast TV and the internet to be experienced simultaneously. This was a step towards blending traditional TV with interactive web content.

Tivo

- Mike Ramsay and Jim Barton: TiVo, co-founded by Ramsay and Barton, revolutionized how we watch TV with its digital recording. Over time, they also integrated internet-based content, thereby blending the TV and internet experiences.

ReplayTV

- Another early competitor to TiVo, ReplayTV offered digital TV recording and also looked to integrate internet features.

The convergence of the internet and TV was seen by many as the next big thing, and various tech industry leaders and companies sought to position themselves at the vanguard of this movement. While not all ventures were successful, they all contributed to the broader vision of a more integrated digital entertainment and information experience.

Social beginnings

I WAS TORN WHETHER to have this in the book or not as I sort of always thought social started"I was on the fence about including this anecdote since I've always associated the social media boom with the period after the dotcom bubble. However, I can't forget the pioneering UK platform, Friends Reunited, that made its mark in 2000. Recalling it just brings a grin to my face, reminding me of a hilarious incident that also serves as a testament to how gullible we were about online profiles.

So here's the scoop: It was 2001, and my buddy, Kevin Doyle, had made a tidy exit from his company and was living the dream in Belgium. He mentioned an upcoming school reunion, and after a few too many Leffe beers (whose idea was it to have that many?), we decided to craft a Friends Reunited profile for him. I say we, it was more just me. And by 'craft,' I mean fabricate a life that was far from the successful reality he was living. With a mischievous click of the 'save' button and a password change for good measure, our version of Kevin's life was now part of the World Wide Web.

Days passed, and the prank faded from memory. But not for long. Kevin soon encountered someone who'd seen that exaggerated profile and expressed sympathy for the unfortunate turn his life had supposedly taken. Whether Kevin ever attended that reunion is still a mystery to me.

This anecdote, while perhaps a 'you-had-to-be-there' kind of funny, underscores the early days of our digital footprints. It's fascinating how a made-up online profile back then is almost akin to the plethora of details we willingly share today. As I write this, a shoutout to Kevin: Sorry mate, but recalling this always gives me a good laugh and I think I may have put you off social media forever.

Friends Reunited: The Spark of Social Connection

LONG BEFORE THE BLUE thumbs of Facebook or the glitz of MySpace profiles, there was a quiet digital revolution unfolding in the UK. It began with a platform that felt more like a cozy school reunion than a sprawling social network. This was Friends Reunited.

Founded in 2000 by Steve and Julie Pankhurst, along with their friend Jason Porter, Friends Reunited was birthed from a simple idea: what if you could reconnect with your old schoolmates online? They created a platform where users could register and find classmates by entering their school's name and graduation year. In the days of a still-maturing internet, the platform was groundbreaking, not just in its concept but in its execution.

Within a year, it exploded in popularity. The initial membership grew exponentially, and by 2003, over 15 million users had joined, a number unheard of for such niche platforms at the time. Its success was partially due to its timing; it tapped into the nostalgia of those who grew up in the 70s and 80s, offering a bridge between the analogue past and the digital present.

Enter MySpace: The Global Playground

While Friends Reunited was capturing hearts in the UK, across the pond, another revolution was brewing. MySpace, launched in 2003 by Chris DeWolfe and Tom Anderson, wasn't just about reconnecting with past schoolmates. It was about expressing yourself, showcasing your taste in music, and, most importantly, expanding your social circle. With its customizable profiles, glittering graphics, and a space for your 'Top 8 friends', MySpace rapidly outpaced Friends Reunited in global recognition and user base.

MySpace was louder, flashier, and designed for the burgeoning youth of the early 2000s. Bands used it to gain popularity, while teenagers flocked to the platform to connect with friends and flaunt their personalities. By 2005, MySpace had dethroned other web giants, becoming the most visited website in the U.S., an accolade that spoke to its meteoric rise.

Facebook: From Ivy Leagues to Global Dominance

But even as MySpace was basking in its limelight, a new contender was silently plotting its ascent. Facebook, started in 2004 by Mark Zuckerberg and his college roommates, initially served a singular purpose: connect Harvard students. But the idea quickly expanded to other Ivy League schools, then all US colleges, and eventually, the world.

What set Facebook apart was its focus on authenticity. While MySpace encouraged flashy personas, Facebook demanded real names and genuine connections. The clean, uniform design of Facebook profiles was a stark contrast to the bedazzled pages of MySpace. It presented a more curated and mature space, appealing to a broader demographic.

Facebook's introduction of the News Feed in 2006 was game-changing. It not only transformed the user experience but also set a precedent for how social media platforms would operate in the future. By 2008, Facebook had overtaken MySpace in terms of unique worldwide visitors, marking the start of its reign as the king of social media.

The Aftermath: Friends Reunited's Decline

AMID THESE RAPID DEVELOPMENTS, Friends Reunited struggled to maintain its momentum. While it had been innovative in its heyday, by the mid-2000s, it seemed antiquated next to the dynamic environments of MySpace and Facebook.

Attempts to monetize the site, like charging users to send messages, drove many away. Simultaneously, Facebook's expanding features, such as Groups and Pages, allowed users to form communities based on interests, workplaces, or educational institutions, essentially integrating the core offering of Friends Reunited.

By 2009, Friends Reunited's user base had dwindled drastically, prompting its sale for a fraction of its peak valuation. It was a sobering moment that highlighted the swift and ruthless nature of technological evolution.

Friends Reunited, MySpace, and Facebook each played pivotal roles in the evolution of social media. While Friends Reunited paved the way for online reconnections, MySpace injected personality into our digital lives, and Facebook universalized and refined the concept of online social networking.

The journey of these platforms offers invaluable lessons. It speaks to the need for constant innovation, adaptability, and understanding users' shifting desires. As the adage goes, 'adapt or perish', and in the digital realm, this has never been truer.

Note 1 - Friends Reunited was never floated but was purchased by ITV for £120m but was sold by 2009 for a fraction of the price

Note 2 - MySpace was purchased by NewCorp for $500m but again dwindled in numbers and purchased by Specific Media ground and justin timberlake for $35m.

Note 3- Facebook IPO for $104bn. Today now known as Meta it's valued at $785bn (price 10th August 2023)

Linkedin, Facebook, MySpace all owe SixDegress

SIXDEGREES, RING A bell? I thought not but SixDegrees was a real pioneer of social back in the late 90s. Before Facebook, before MySpace, even before Friendster, there was SixDegrees. It was one of the very first online platforms that aimed to digitally recreate and utilize real-world social networks. For many internet users of the late 1990s, SixDegrees was their introduction to the concept of online social networking.

The Rise:

FOUNDED IN 1997 BY Andrew Weinreich, SixDegrees was named after the "six degrees of separation" concept, which posits that any two people in the world are, on average, separated by no more than six social connections. The platform allowed users to create profiles, list their friends and acquaintances, and then view their connections in a visual web of relationships. Users could send messages, establish connections, and even see how they were linked to strangers.

In a world before the ubiquity of smartphones and broadband internet, SixDegrees was ahead of its time. The idea was revolutionary: harness the power of the internet to map and explore personal relationships.

By 1999, the platform boasted a user base of around 3.5 million members. The rapid growth and unique proposition made it a darling of the dotcom era, attracting significant investor attention and funding.

The Fall:

HOWEVER, AS WITH MANY startups during the dotcom boom, rapid growth came with its own set of challenges. Several factors contributed to the decline of SixDegrees:

> User Experience: The platform faced scalability issues. As user numbers grew, the site often became slow and unresponsive.
>
> Monetization: While SixDegrees had a large user base, turning those users into revenue proved challenging. Advertisements were the primary revenue source, but they weren't as lucrative as hoped.
>
> Privacy Concerns: The idea of publicly listing one's personal relationships was still novel, and many users were hesitant about sharing such information broadly. Privacy controls were rudimentary compared to today's standards.
>
> Competition: As the internet grew, so did competition. Other platforms began to emerge with similar or improved functionalities.
>
> Dotcom Bubble Burst: The economic downturn of the early 2000s, often referred to as the bursting of the "dotcom bubble," affected many online startups, including SixDegrees.

By December 2000, just three years after its launch, SixDegrees was shut down. While the company had tried to pivot and find new avenues for revenue, including a paid subscription model, these efforts were insufficient to save it.

Legacy:

DESPITE ITS RELATIVELY short lifespan, SixDegrees left an indelible mark on the world of online social networking. It demonstrated the public's interest in digitally mapping and exploring their personal relationships. The challenges faced by SixDegrees provided lessons for future platforms, many of which took the concept and refined it.

Future social networking giants, from Friendster and MySpace to LinkedIn and Facebook, owe a debt to SixDegrees. While they may have refined the model and expanded on the concept, SixDegrees was undeniably one of the pioneers, providing a glimpse into the potential of online connectivity long before it became a staple of modern life.

Note : SixDegrees never held a IPO and raised $25m during its time.

Unforgettable Fails of the Dotcom Era: The Cautionary Tale of Pets.com

IN THE DIZZYING HEIGHTS of the Dotcom boom, optimism was infectious. There were almost 500 tech companies that held IPOs, riding the wave of innovation and speculative investment. While this era heralded some legendary successes, it also witnessed spectacular failures that remain etched in business lore. These tales serve as cautionary reminders about the importance of sustainable growth and the dangers of unchecked ambition.

One of the era's most iconic implosions was Pets.com. Although it wasn't as publicized in Europe, its presence was ubiquitous in the US, thanks in no small part to its infamous sock puppet mascot. The puppet was not just a marketing tool; it became emblematic of the company's exorbitant spending. For every dollar the company earned, they were spending multiples on advertising.

Founded by entrepreneur Greg McLemore, who previously spearheaded Toys.com, Pets.com was more than just a business to him—it was a dream. Backed by heavyweight investors, including Amazon and Hummer Winblad Venture Partners, the company aimed to be the digital answer to the pet supply industry. They believed the internet would redefine commerce, and they intended to be at the forefront of this revolution.

However, this ambitious vision soon met with reality. In the heady days of the Dotcom bubble, Pets.com expanded with fervor but without a clear profitability strategy. The company faced inherent challenges in e-commerce logistics. Shipping bulky and heavy items like pet food was not only logistically challenging but also expensive. This was a time before the likes of Amazon Prime had revolutionized e-commerce delivery. The company often sold products at a loss, hoping to gain on volume—a strategy that, while popular during that era, was fundamentally flawed for Pets.com.

Reflecting on the downfall, founder Greg McLemore cited a confluence of factors. From the broader market crash, logistic nightmares, to being perhaps too ahead of its time, the deck was stacked against Pets.com. He has since remarked, "We were pioneering an entirely new realm of shopping, and with that came the challenges of educating the market."

While McLemore continued his journey in the entrepreneurial world, Pets.com stands as a poignant reminder from the Dotcom era. It symbolizes the balance between vision and viability, serving as a testament to the perils of rapid expansion without a clear and sustainable business model.

Unforgettable Fails of the Dotcom Era: The Rise and Fall of TheGlobe.com

IN THE ANNALS OF DOTCOM history, certain narratives stand out not just for their spectacular rises, but also for their precipitous falls. Among the glittering constellation of early internet startups was TheGlobe.com, a pioneer in the realm of social networking long before the likes of Facebook or Twitter entered the scene.

Founded by two Cornell students, Stephan Paternot and Todd Krizelman, in 1994, TheGlobe.com was a platform that allowed users to create their own customizable web pages and interact with others. This was a novel concept at a time when the internet was still in its infancy. The idea was born out of their dorm room, and it burgeoned into one of the earliest online communities, giving a platform for people to connect, share, and express themselves.

TheGlobe.com's ascent to fame was meteoric. In November 1998, the company went public, and its IPO became the stuff of legend. On its first trading day, the stock price skyrocketed, opening at $9 and closing at $63.50, marking a 600% increase and setting an IPO record. With a valuation nearing a billion dollars, the future looked incredibly bright for TheGlobe.com.

But this euphoria was not to last. TheGlobe.com's business model was heavily reliant on advertising revenue. While it had a massive user base, converting those users into sustainable profits proved elusive. As the Dotcom bubble started to show cracks, investors grew wary of companies that showed great promise but lacked a clear path to profitability.

And then came the challenges. The competitive landscape became more crowded. Larger entities with deeper pockets began to emerge, offering similar or superior services. Additionally, issues like unsolicited spamming on their platform tainted TheGlobe.com's reputation.

Reflecting on the company's trajectory, co-founder Stephan Paternot often acknowledged the rapid pace at which everything transpired. "We were at the forefront of something monumental, but we were also learning on the go. There were no playbooks," he once remarked.

The Dotcom crash of the early 2000s was the final nail in the coffin. In 2001, facing a shrinking user base and mounting financial pressures, TheGlobe.com ceased many of its operations. By 2008, the company had completely dissolved.

Today, TheGlobe.com is remembered as an emblematic tale of the Dotcom era

Unforgettable Fails of the Dotcom Era: The Rise and Fall of Go.com

THE DOTCOM BOOM WAS marked by its ambitious projects, rapid growth, and its spectacular implosions. Among the giants that tried their hands at dominating the internet landscape was Disney, with its venture: Go.com.

Established in the late 1990s, Go.com was Disney's attempt to create a comprehensive web portal and search engine, leveraging its vast media properties and resources. The idea was ambitious: a one-stop online destination where users could access news, entertainment, and search, all with the magic touch of Disney.

From its inception, Go.com faced stiff competition. It was entering an already crowded marketplace, vying against established players like Yahoo, Lycos, and Excite. Undeterred, Disney hoped that by integrating its vast entertainment content, including ABC and ESPN properties, it could carve out a unique niche for Go.com.

However, the journey was riddled with challenges. The platform underwent multiple redesigns in its short lifespan. Initially, Go.com tried to differentiate itself with a unique green traffic light cursor, which was eventually dropped due to usability concerns. The integration of so many diverse Disney assets into a cohesive user experience also proved daunting.

While Go.com did garner a significant number of users, thanks in part to Disney's marketing muscle, it struggled with identity. Was it primarily an entertainment portal? A search engine? A hub for Disney aficionados? This lack of clear direction and purpose hampered its potential.

WEB 1.0 DOTCOM ERA DEFINED 45

The nail in the coffin was the bursting of the Dotcom bubble. As the internet landscape dramatically shifted and online advertising revenues tanked, the economic viability of Go.com became questionable. Recognizing the challenges, Disney started to scale back its aspirations for the portal. By early 2001, the company announced it would be phasing out the Go.com brand as an independent entity, instead focusing on leveraging its content properties separately on the web.

Reflecting on Go.com, many analysts and tech historians opine that while Disney had the resources and content for a successful portal, its execution and timing were off. Trying to enter a saturated market without a clear unique selling proposition was a recipe for challenges.

Today, Go.com exists primarily as the web portal for Disney's ESPN, a shadow of its initial grand ambition.

Unforgettable Fails of the Dotcom Era: The Rise and Fall of AltaVista

AMIDST THE CACOPHONY of the Dotcom boom, there emerged a star: AltaVista. For those who navigated the early digital realms, AltaVista was more than just a name; it was the portal to the vast world of the internet. As I delved deeper into this iconic brand for my research, a wave of nostalgia hit. It wasn't just any search engine; it was a platform I, along with countless others, turned to frequently.

AltaVista's journey began in 1995, birthed in the labs of Digital Equipment Corporation (DEC) by Dr. Louis Monier and Michael Burrows. Their ambition was to create a search engine that could index a significant chunk of the burgeoning web, and in that, they succeeded splendidly. Unlike its peers, AltaVista indexed an extensive portion of the web, quickly setting the standard for what an efficient search engine should be.

Early adopters were not only impressed by its sheer indexing capabilities but also by the innovative features it introduced. Natural language queries, and the ability to search for images, video, and audio, were groundbreaking for their time.

Yet, as is often the case with pioneers, the road was fraught with challenges. Despite its early prominence, AltaVista struggled to maintain its leading position as the internet landscape evolved. Google, a newer entrant, began its inexorable rise, offering a minimalistic design and an algorithm that constantly improved itself.

The 2000s were unkind to AltaVista. After being acquired by Compaq in 1998, it went through several ownership changes. Each transition attempted to redefine AltaVista, often cluttering its interface with ads and detracting from the user experience.

In reflection, Dr. Louis Monier, one of its founders, remarked in interviews over the years about the changing priorities and missed opportunities that contributed to AltaVista's decline. He noted how the company got caught up in features and lost focus on refining the core search experience, a domain where Google excelled.

As for its financial journey, AltaVista did make strides towards an IPO, hoping to raise a significant capital infusion. However, those plans were shelved when Compaq acquired the company. The exact numbers remain part of the era's lore, with many speculating on what might have been had AltaVista gone public in its prime.

By the time 2003 rolled around, Yahoo took ownership of AltaVista and, in a move that marked the end of an era, shut it down in 2013.

AltaVista's story serves as a powerful reminder in the tech world. Innovation and early success do not guarantee longevity. But for many of us who were active during its peak, AltaVista will always be fondly remembered as a pioneer that helped shape the early contours of the digital world.

Unforgettable Fails of the Dotcom Era: The Rise and Fall of Ask Jeeves

AH, ASK JEEVES! A PERSONAL favorite of mine from the Dotcom boom. Whenever I think of it, the imagery of a dapper butler ready to answer all your queries comes to mind, thanks to their memorable advertising campaign. Particularly in the UK, I vividly recall their extensive promotional efforts featuring the iconic butler, making the platform instantly recognizable.

Launching in 1996, Ask Jeeves was the brainchild of Garrett Gruener and David Warthen. It was designed to allow users to pose queries in natural language, a novel approach at the time. The platform was meant to replicate the experience of asking a knowledgeable individual (Jeeves, the butler) any question. The idea was both innovative and intuitive, and for many users, it presented a friendly interface in the vast and often bewildering landscape of the early internet.

In its heyday, Ask Jeeves had a significant user base and saw an impressive uptake, especially in the UK. Its intuitive query system appealed to many who found traditional search engines' keyword-based searches cumbersome.

However, the path of internet pioneers is rarely smooth. As the new millennium dawned, Google started its ascent, introducing a simple, effective search algorithm and a clean interface that quickly won users over. Ask Jeeves' unique selling point—the natural language query—was being overshadowed by the sheer efficiency and precision of Google's results.

To its credit, Ask Jeeves did attempt several reinventions. It dropped "Jeeves" from its branding in 2005, becoming just "Ask.com."

But it struggled to find a niche that would differentiate it from its rising competitors.

Reflecting on its trajectory, Gruener and Warthen have over the years indicated that while the platform had a unique value proposition, perhaps it wasn't agile enough to adapt to the rapidly changing internet landscape. The insinuation being, perhaps, that while they carved a unique space in the search engine market, they might have underestimated the pace at which the internet would evolve and the emergence of dominant players like Google.

Financially, Ask Jeeves had its moment in the sun. The company went public in 1999, riding the Dotcom wave. It managed to raise significant capital, showcasing the market's faith in its potential. However, just as the sun sets, the initial enthusiasm waned as challenges mounted.

The story of Ask Jeeves is a poignant one. While it's remembered fondly by many (including me) as a pioneering platform, it's also a tale of how even the most promising and innovative ventures can be overshadowed in the fast-paced world of tech. The butler might have retired, but for those of us who were there during its zenith, Ask Jeeves will always hold a special place in our digital memories.

Unforgettable Chronicles of the Dotcom Era: The Tale of FuckedCompany.com

IN THE EXHILARATING and often tumultuous world of the Dotcom boom, where companies both sprouted and shuttered at dizzying rates, there loomed a platform that epitomized the zeitgeist of that era: FuckedCompany.com. Yes, you read that name right. And the story behind it is as intriguing as its bold title.

The brainchild of Philip "Pud" Kaplan, FuckedCompany.com was launched in 2000. Kaplan, an entrepreneur and developer, created the platform initially as a half-joke, but its resonance with the Dotcom audience turned it into a cult favorite. With its audacious name and even more audacious content, the site quickly carved out a reputation for itself.

Personally, I held a deep appreciation for this platform. Beyond the shock value of its name, it was its substance that had me, and many others, hooked. In an era where corporate narratives were often doused in PR fluff, FuckedCompany.com offered a brutally honest, unfiltered peek behind the curtain.

Tech aficionados, wary investors, and industry insiders alike frequented the site. From the leak of spicy internal emails to the exposure of confidential corporate documents, from wild rumors to inconvenient truths, everything was on display. And yes, even Commerce One had its moments under this unsparing spotlight. It seemed no tech entity in Silicon Valley was safe from FuckedCompany.com's reach.

Yet, beyond the gossip and revelations, the platform also served as a stark reflection of corporate culture. It unveiled the human stories behind those polished corporate façades, often tales of aspirations, deceptions, and sometimes, redemptions.

Given its popularity, you might wonder: what led to its decline? As with many things in the fast-paced Dotcom world, sustainability proved elusive. The initial allure of the site, its rawness, became its Achilles heel. As the Dotcom bubble burst and the tech world matured, the demand for such no-holds-barred platforms began to wane. Moreover, legal challenges, often from companies displeased with their portrayal, plagued the site. By 2007, Kaplan decided to shutter FuckedCompany.com, marking the end of an iconic chapter in internet history.

Looking back, the essence of FuckedCompany.com — its spirit of unapologetic transparency — feels more relevant than ever in today's corporate climate. As information flows freely in our digital age, one can't help but ponder if there's room for a revival of such a platform. After all, in any era, there remains an insatiable appetite for the untold stories lurking behind those gleaming corporate logos.

Business-to-Business (B2B) Dotcoms

Commerce One: A Visionary in B2B E-commerce

HAD TO HAVE THIS INCLUDED in here but as I previously said it deserves its own books.

If I was asked why Commerce One failed in the end it would be the stuff we know about with the whole Dotcom thing, but it would also be the SAP warrants and the loss of Thomas Gonzlas Junior.

In the luminous tapestry of the Dotcom era, there are narratives that shine brightly, casting both illuminating successes and elongated shadows of ambition. Among these stories is the saga of Commerce One, a company that aimed to redefine the boundaries of B2B e-commerce.

The brainchild of Mark Hoffman and Tom Gonzales, Commerce One was conceived in the fervor of the late 90s, a time when the digital landscape was rapidly transforming, and the possibilities seemed boundless. Mark Hoffman, who previously had a long stint at Sybase, an enterprise software company, brought with him an acute understanding of the challenges and opportunities in the enterprise sector.

The vision was simple yet revolutionary: to create an online marketplace for businesses, where goods and services could be traded seamlessly. They wanted to eliminate the intricacies and inefficiencies of traditional procurement processes by leveraging the power of the internet. However, the challenge was massive. Unlike consumer-focused platforms, B2B interactions involved a plethora of stakeholders, intricate transaction processes, and colossal amounts of data.

From the start, Commerce One was seen as more than just a startup. Their initial product, a procurement application launched in 1997, quickly gained traction, marking their first step into the world of electronic marketplaces. This product simplified the procurement process for businesses, allowing for smoother negotiations, transparent pricing, and a reduction in the paperwork that had long burdened companies.

In 1999, their aspirations took a leap with the introduction of Commerce One MarketSite, a global trading portal meant to serve as a hub for businesses to not just procure, but also to sell their products and services. This move positioned Commerce One at the forefront of the B2B e-commerce revolution.

But as with many stories from this era, success wasn't solely defined by innovation. The backdrop of the late 90s, with its easy capital and exuberant investor sentiment, played its role. Commerce One's narrative was punctuated with rapid expansions, high-profile partnerships, and a stock price that, at one point, defied gravity.

Behind the scenes, Hoffman and Gonzales were a perfect blend of pragmatism and vision. While Hoffman, with his software background, was rooted in the technical and operational aspects, Gonzales brought with him an expansive network and a flair for strategic partnerships.

SAP and Commerce One: A Partnership Turned Pitfall

COMMERCE ONE'S AMBITIONS were grand and its trajectory seemed unstoppable, especially after its dazzling initial public offering in 1999. With the B2B market booming and investors hungry for anything with a ".com" in its title, Commerce One's stock soared.

However, even the most promising narratives in business can sometimes be marked by miscalculations, and for Commerce One, a significant turn came in the form of its alliance with SAP, the German software giant.

SAP, a titan in the enterprise resource planning (ERP) space, saw the growing potential of e-commerce and was eager to tap into the burgeoning market. In Commerce One, it saw not just a ticket to this new arena, but a partner whose e-marketplace platform could complement its own strengths in enterprise software.

In 2000, the two companies announced a strategic alliance. On the surface, the partnership was poised for success. SAP invested $250 million into Commerce One and the duo jointly developed SAP Markets, aiming to leverage each other's strengths. SAP's vast global customer base seemed to promise a ready market for Commerce One's solutions, while SAP hoped to expand its horizons beyond its traditional ERP base.

However, the devil, as they say, was in the details.

One of the sticking points in the partnership was the issue of stock warrants. SAP's investment came with attached warrants that gave it the right to purchase additional Commerce One shares at a predetermined price. As Commerce One's stock began its roller-coaster ride in the volatile market, these warrants became a significant financial instrument, one that would eventually spell trouble for Commerce One.

When the tech bubble burst, Commerce One's stock price plummeted, and the value of these warrants dropped dramatically. This would have been a regular financial misstep in most scenarios, but given the size and implication of the deal with SAP, it magnified Commerce One's financial troubles.

But financial mechanics aside, there were operational challenges too. The integration of two companies, especially of such different sizes and from different continents, was no easy feat. There were inevitable clashes in corporate cultures, strategies, and visions for the future. Moreover, the promised synergy from the collaboration - the rapid customer expansion and integrated product capabilities - did not materialize as smoothly as anticipated.

An additional blow came with the departure of Tom Gonzales Jr., a pivotal figure in Commerce One's ascent. His exit left a vacuum, one that was felt deeply given the challenges the company was facing.

Reflecting on the downfall, it's clear that while the SAP partnership promised much, it delivered little in terms of sustained strategic advantage. The combination of financial complications, integration challenges, and a rapidly changing market landscape proved too much for Commerce One.

Commerce One's Covisint: Revolutionizing the Automotive Industry

THE AUTOMOTIVE INDUSTRY, known for its vast supply chains, intricate networks, and decades-old relationships between suppliers and manufacturers, stood on the brink of a digital transformation at the turn of the millennium. Sensing an opportunity, Commerce One, with its reputation in e-commerce solutions and B2B marketplaces, stepped onto the scene with a vision: to reshape the way automakers and suppliers interacted. The result was Covisint, a platform designed to revolutionize the automotive supply chain.

Jointly developed with the collaboration of major automotive giants like General Motors, Ford, and DaimlerChrysler, Covisint aimed to serve as a centralized digital marketplace. The platform's promise was clear: to bring unprecedented efficiency, transparency, and speed to an industry where communication, procurement, and partnership processes had remained largely unchanged for decades.

Covisint intended to simplify the procurement process for automakers. Instead of having multiple conversations with countless suppliers, automakers could now access a centralized platform where they could streamline their interactions, handle transactions, and manage their relationships. For suppliers, Covisint offered a chance to bid on contracts, connect with multiple automakers, and gain insights into industry trends and demands, all within a single digital environment.

The potential benefits were enormous. Cost savings from streamlined processes, reduced errors in procurement, faster response times to market changes, and the ability to foster more dynamic, real-time collaborations between manufacturers and suppliers.

However, implementing such a transformative vision in an industry steeped in tradition was no easy task. The challenges were manifold. For one, the automotive industry had a deeply embedded culture and decades-long relationships built on trust and personal interactions. Convincing industry veterans to shift to a digital-first approach required more than just showcasing the platform's technical capabilities. It needed a change in mindset.

There was also the sheer complexity of integrating with existing IT systems. With numerous legacy systems in place across different companies, ensuring that Covisint could seamlessly integrate and function without disruptions was paramount.

Moreover, while Covisint was groundbreaking, it wasn't without competition. Other digital platforms and marketplaces began to emerge, vying for the attention of automakers and suppliers, leading to a fragmented landscape.

Despite these challenges, Covisint made notable inroads into the automotive industry, garnering significant attention and attracting a range of users to its platform. It symbolized the future of the automotive supply chain, even if the industry wasn't entirely ready to embrace it.

Role of B2B in the dotcom bubble

THE DOTCOM BUBBLE IS often remembered for its B2C (Business-to-Consumer) excesses, but the B2B (Business-to-Business) sector played a significant, if somewhat less publicized, role in both the rise and the fall of the era.

Rapid Growth and High Expectations: At the height of the Dotcom boom, B2B was seen as the next frontier of the internet revolution. Projections about the potential of B2B e-commerce were astronomical, with some analysts predicting that by 2003, B2B transactions would surpass $7 trillion. Companies and investors flocked to the B2B space, expecting it to be the next gold mine.

Emergence of Online Marketplaces: One of the defining features of the B2B Dotcom era was the rise of online marketplaces. These platforms, like Commerce One and Ariba, aimed to connect buyers and suppliers in a seamless digital environment, promising efficiencies and cost savings.

Overcapitalization and Competition: With the allure of the B2B market potential, startups in the space often received massive capital infusions. This influx of money, while enabling growth, also led to saturated markets. Multiple companies offered similar solutions, which diluted the value proposition and increased customer acquisition costs.

Technological Challenges: While the vision of seamless online B2B marketplaces was compelling, the reality was often messier. Integrating disparate IT systems between companies, ensuring transaction security, and handling the sheer volume of potential B2B transactions posed significant technical challenges.

Slow Adoption: Contrary to B2C sectors, B2B involves long-standing relationships, complex decision-making processes, and often, larger transaction volumes. Companies were hesitant to shift their operations to newly established online platforms, leading to slower than anticipated adoption rates.

The Burst and Aftermath: When the bubble burst, B2B companies were hit hard. The vast projections did not materialize as quickly as anticipated. Overextended companies faced a harsh reality, leading to closures, layoffs, and consolidations. Yet, it wasn't all doom and gloom. The foundational ideas behind B2B e-commerce were sound, and post-bubble, the sector saw a more measured, sustainable growth.

Legacy of the B2B Boom: Despite the tumultuous times, the Dotcom era did lay the groundwork for the future of B2B. Lessons were learned about the importance of truly understanding customer needs, the risks of overextension, and the need for sustainable, value-driven growth. Today, B2B e-commerce is a thriving industry, benefiting from the early pioneers of the Dotcom era, even if their initial visions were ahead of their time.

The Role of Venture Capital

Sequoia, Kleiner Perkins, Benchmark: Betting big.

SEQUOIA CAPITAL, ONE of the most prestigious venture capital firms in the world, played an instrumental role during the Dotcom boom. Their influence in the late 1990s and early 2000s wasn't just limited to their investments; it also extended to the advice they offered, the companies they nurtured, and the overall impact they had on Silicon Valley's entrepreneurial ecosystem. Here's a closer look at Sequoia's role during the Dotcom era:

Picking Winners Early: Sequoia had an uncanny ability to spot promising startups early on. Companies like Google, Yahoo!, and PayPal received early-stage funding from Sequoia, proving the firm's forward-thinking approach and ability to discern potential in a sea of Dotcom startups.

Influential Guidance: Sequoia wasn't just a passive investor. They were known for their hands-on approach, offering strategic guidance, connecting founders with their vast network, and helping startups navigate the often-tumultuous waters of the Dotcom era.

Weathering the Storm: The Dotcom bubble burst had a profound impact on many VC firms, some of which didn't survive. Sequoia, however, managed to weather the storm. While some of their investments certainly suffered, their diverse portfolio and prudent investment strategy ensured they remained a dominant force in the venture capital space.

Crazy Deals: Like most VC firms of the time, Sequoia was involved in some deals that, in hindsight, may seem overzealous or misguided given the frothy nature of the Dotcom era. One of the more controversial decisions was the rapid pace at which funding rounds occurred, sometimes within months of each other, and at significantly inflated valuations.

Advisory Role: Sequoia was not just about funding. Their partners were known for their mentoring and advisory roles. A famous instance is the "R.I.P. Good Times" presentation in 2008, where Sequoia warned its portfolio companies of the impending economic downturn and advised them on survival strategies. While this came after the Dotcom burst, it's indicative of the advisory role Sequoia has played historically.

Shift in Strategy: The aftermath of the Dotcom bust led many VC firms, including Sequoia, to reevaluate their investment strategies. There was a marked shift towards more sustainable business models and a greater emphasis on profitability rather than just growth and user acquisition.

In essence, Sequoia's role in the Dotcom boom was multifaceted. They were instrumental in funding and guiding some of the era's most significant success stories, but like many, they also faced challenges when the bubble burst. Their enduring legacy, however, is a testament to their adaptability, foresight, and deep-rooted understanding of the tech startup landscape.

Kleiner Perkins and the Dotcom Dance

SILICON VALLEY, THE global hub of technological innovation, was in a state of fervor as the 1990s drew to a close. A new digital frontier was unfolding, promising unprecedented opportunities. Venture capitalists, the high-stake gamblers of the tech world, were eager to place their bets. Among them stood a titan, Kleiner Perkins, ready to dive into the Dotcom dance with gusto.

Kleiner Perkins wasn't new to the scene. Founded in 1972, they'd already etched their names into the annals of tech history with a portfolio that boasted of early-stage investments in companies that had grown into giants. But the Dotcom era was unlike any other. The internet, a platform that was perceived to have transformative potential, offered chances to redefine industries, making it a playground for visionary investors.

However, this new playground came with its own set of rules. The rapid pace of the Dotcom era meant decisions had to be made swiftly. While Kleiner Perkins had a knack for spotting stars, their portfolio from this period was a mixed bag. Amazon and Netscape shone brightly, testament to their visionary bets. But shadows lurked in the form of investments like Excite@Home and Kozmo - reminders of the inherent risks of the game.

An interesting phenomenon arose during this period, the "KP Effect". Such was the charisma of Kleiner Perkins that their mere association with a startup often acted like a seal of credibility. This effect meant easier access to additional funding, talent acquisition, and even media attention for the funded startups. But this allure also had its pitfalls. The seductive dance of the Dotcom era sometimes led even seasoned players like Kleiner Perkins astray. They found themselves backing companies with unproven business models, captivated by the internet's siren song.

Tensions simmered within the firm too. The Dotcom mania brought with it disagreements among partners. Some were concerned that the firm's storied legacy was at risk, as it veered towards internet-related investments, sidelining traditional tech opportunities.

Then, the music stopped. The bubble burst, leaving behind a trail of shattered dreams and bankrupt startups. But like any seasoned dancer, Kleiner Perkins took a moment, caught their breath, and began their next act. A period of introspection ensued. They revisited their strategies, sifting through the lessons from the Dotcom era. Their focus pivoted, encompassing not just tech but also fields like green technology and life sciences.

Their legacy during the Dotcom era wasn't just about the money they poured into companies. It was about shaping the cultural fabric of Silicon Valley. They championed the spirit of innovation, risk-taking, and entrepreneurship, qualities that defined the era.

In the vast tapestry of the Dotcom boom and bust, Kleiner Perkins stands out not just as a participant but as a maestro, orchestrating some of its most memorable tunes. Their journey through the Dotcom era serves as a testament to the delicate dance between vision, risk, and resilience in the ever-evolving world of technology.

Benchmark and the Dotcom Symphony

IN THE GRAND ORCHESTRA of the Dotcom era, various players held pivotal roles. And while the sounds of the Silicon Valley crescendo grew louder and more harmonious at times, some players managed to set themselves apart with a distinctive note. Benchmark, a venture capital firm founded in 1995, was one such maestro that played the Dotcom symphony with a unique flair.

From the outset, Benchmark distinguished itself from its peers. Unlike the hierarchical structures prevalent in most venture capital firms, Benchmark prided itself on an egalitarian ethos. Each partner at Benchmark held equal weight, and their investments weren't just about capital – they were handshakes of trust, symbolizing partnerships in the truest sense.

As the Dotcom frenzy began, Benchmark was quick to recognize the promise and peril it held. Their early bets reflected a discerning eye. One of their most notable successes was eBay, an online auction platform which, at the time, was but a nascent idea in the vast sea of internet possibilities. That investment not only yielded phenomenal returns but also firmly established Benchmark's reputation as a force to be reckoned with in the venture capital world.

However, the Dotcom era was as much about spectacular misses as it was about home runs. Benchmark, despite their successes, was not immune to the siren song of the internet age. They made investments that, in hindsight, were overly optimistic, perhaps emblematic of the general euphoria that permeated the Silicon Valley.

Yet, what set Benchmark apart was their commitment to the entrepreneurial spirit. They weren't just silent financiers; they were collaborators. Startups backed by Benchmark often spoke of the invaluable guidance they received, be it in the form of strategy formulation, network-building, or navigating the tumultuous waters of the Dotcom boom and bust.

The landscape was fraught with challenges, and many venture capitalists were drawn into the speculative mania. As the Dotcom bubble expanded, the sheer volume of investments and the dizzying valuations became hard to justify. And when the bubble inevitably burst, the aftermath was sobering. Startups folded overnight, dreams were shattered, and a general air of caution replaced the earlier optimism.

For Benchmark, the Dotcom era was a period of highs and lows. Yet, their story is not one of mere survival, but of resilience and evolution. Post the Dotcom bust, they re-calibrated, drawing from their experiences to make more informed bets in the subsequent years.

Benchmark's journey during the Dotcom era serves as a lesson in humility and adaptability. Their legacy from this period isn't just in the companies they backed, but in the manner in which they navigated the highs and lows, remaining steadfast in their commitment to innovation, entrepreneurial spirit, and a belief in the transformative power of technology. Their notes in the Dotcom symphony may have varied in pitch and tone, but they always added to the ensemble, enriching the collective melody of an unforgettable era.

Music & Media Streaming Beginnings

Napster - The Unconventional Symphony of the Digital Age

THE DOTCOM ERA WAS a symphony of innovations, each player adding a unique note to the evolving composition. Some notes, however, resonated more profoundly than others, creating ripples that forever altered the digital soundscape. One such transformative melody emerged from an unconventional source: Napster.

Founded in 1999 by Shawn Fanning, Napster was more than just a product of the Dotcom zeitgeist; it was a revolutionary idea that heralded a new era in music distribution. Fanning, a college dropout with an innate knack for coding, conceived Napster not out of grand ambitions but from a personal itch. Frustrated with the existing methods of finding and sharing music online, he envisioned a platform where individuals could easily share their music collections.

The premise was simple: a peer-to-peer file-sharing service that allowed users to share music files with others. However, its impact was profound. Almost overnight, Napster gained an immense following. College students, music enthusiasts, and even those unfamiliar with the intricacies of the internet were drawn to this novel idea. It wasn't just a platform; it was a movement.

Behind Napster's meteoric rise was Fanning's background. Unlike many Silicon Valley prodigies groomed in elite institutions, Fanning's journey was non-linear. He hailed from Brockton, Massachusetts, and grew up amidst financial challenges. His parents divorced early, and he bounced between relatives, finding solace in the world of computers.

This fascination with technology was not just a hobby but an escape, a portal to a world where possibilities seemed limitless.

Napster was a testament to Fanning's ingenuity, but it was also emblematic of a deeper cultural shift. The digital age was democratizing access, challenging established norms, and enabling individuals to reclaim control. The music industry, long dominated by a few major labels, suddenly found its monopoly threatened.

However, revolutions seldom go uncontested. Napster's disruption did not sit well with the music moguls. They viewed Napster not as an evolution but as an existential threat, leading to a slew of legal battles. Artists, too, were divided. Some saw it as piracy, while others viewed it as a new way to connect with fans.

Despite its short lifespan, Napster's legacy endures. It forced the music industry to reckon with the digital age, paving the way for platforms like iTunes, Spotify, and SoundCloud. It exemplified the transformative power of technology, how a simple idea, when met with the right timing and execution, can challenge empires.

The story of Napster and Shawn Fanning is more than just a chapter in the Dotcom saga. It's a reminder of the indomitable human spirit, the belief that individuals, even those from humble beginnings, can shape industries, influence cultures, and forever alter the course of history. In the grand symphony of the digital age, Napster remains one of its most unforgettable melodies.

In the warm embrace of 1999's summer, two visionaries, Shawn Fanning and Sean Parker, quietly sowed the seeds of what would soon morph into a technological behemoth: Napster. With a deceptively simple premise, this peer-to-peer file-sharing service allowed users to freely exchange music files. But beneath this simplicity lay a profound shift in how people would consume music. Within just a year, Napster's user base surged to an astonishing 70 million, accounting for a massive portion of all internet traffic and heralding a new era in digital music.

WEB 1.0 DOTCOM ERA DEFINED 67

But as Napster's star ascended, a storm brewed on the horizon. Its rapid popularity among young and tech-savvy users was matched by rising consternation within the music industry. Iconic bands like Metallica were among the first to raise the battle cry. In 2000, they initiated legal action against Napster after a demo of their song "I Disappear" had prematurely found its way to the platform, getting widely distributed even before its official release. Dr. Dre soon followed suit, his grievance stemming from Napster's refusal to delist his songs.

The crux of the dispute was a complex interplay between innovation and copyright. While the platform itself was a passive conduit, merely facilitating the sharing without hosting the files, many artists felt it eroded the sanctity of their work. The Recording Industry Association of America (RIAA) didn't stand on the sidelines for long, charging Napster with copyright infringement by the close of 1999.

The legal battles took their toll, and by July 2001, a U.S. District Judge's ruling sounded the death knell for the original Napster. The platform was mandated to remain dormant until it could guarantee the absence of copyrighted material. This once potential billion-dollar behemoth's journey culminated in a sobering 2002 bankruptcy filing.

Yet, the essence of Napster persisted, shaping the future contours of the music industry. In its wake, platforms like iTunes and Spotify emerged, adapting to the demands of both technology and legality, ensuring that the music, and its rightful creators, always found their due. The tale of Napster, resplendent in its highs and sobering in its lows, remains an evocative chapter in the annals of the digital age, a testament to the transformative power of innovation and the challenges that accompany it.

In the entwined saga of Napster, one figure stands out with a particular luminance: Sean Parker. Often portrayed with a blend of genius and audacity, Parker co-founded Napster alongside Shawn Fanning when he was barely out of his teenage years. His role in the platform wasn't just that of a co-founder; he was its lifeblood, its beating heart, and often its most vocal champion.

Parker's youthful exuberance and unbridled passion for the potential of the digital realm were palpable. He was instrumental in shaping the platform's direction and was indefatigable in his efforts to secure funds and support for the fledgling company. But with this brilliance came an impetuousness that was as unpredictable as it was magnetic.

Anecdotes about Parker's antics during the Napster days border on the legendary. He was known to oscillate between moments of profound clarity, where he would envision paths forward for the company that others hadn't considered, to periods of unbridled rebellion, challenging the status quo and ruffling more than a few feathers. His charisma was undeniable, drawing both ardent admirers and skeptical critics in equal measure.

But behind this maverick facade was a deep-seated belief in the democratization of music. Parker saw Napster as not just a platform for sharing songs, but as a revolutionary tool that could topple the barriers of traditional music distribution, enabling artists to reach their audience directly. For him, it wasn't merely about free music; it was about a free and interconnected world.

However, as Napster's legal woes deepened, Parker's wild side became both an asset and a liability. His determination kept the team motivated, but his sometimes brash approach to negotiation and publicity often put Napster in the crosshairs of an already antagonistic music industry. By the time the legal battles reached their zenith, Parker had already been ousted from his role at the company. Yet, his influence lingered, with many crediting him for laying the groundwork that would shape the digital music landscape for years to come.

Sean Parker's time at Napster might have been brief, but it was undeniably impactful. The tale of his journey, rife with brilliance, controversy, and unyielding conviction, mirrors the very essence of the dotcom era: tumultuous, groundbreaking, and forever etched in the annals of digital history.

After his tumultuous time with Napster, Sean Parker's journey was far from over. In fact, the best was yet to come. Parker has an uncanny ability to find himself at the intersection of groundbreaking technological shifts, and his subsequent ventures only solidified his reputation as a formidable entrepreneur.

His next notable achievement was the involvement with Plaxo in 2002, an online address book and social networking service that introduced many of the features that would later become standard in the social media world. Through Plaxo, Parker showcased his deep understanding of virality and network effects, employing aggressive tactics to grow its user base.

However, it was his association with Facebook that truly thrust him into the limelight. In 2004, Parker became the first president of Facebook, after serendipitously meeting Mark Zuckerberg and recognizing the platform's immense potential. Under his guidance, Facebook transformed from a college project to a Silicon Valley powerhouse. He played a crucial role in Facebook's early growth and was instrumental in securing its initial outside investment. Parker famously convinced Zuckerberg to turn down multiple buyout offers, persuading him of Facebook's potential to become a multi-billion-dollar platform.

Yet, just as with Napster, Parker's time at Facebook was marred with controversy. He left the company in 2005, following a disagreement with Zuckerberg and investors. However, his early involvement and equity stake in Facebook ensured he reaped significant financial rewards when the company went public.

But Parker, ever the serial entrepreneur, didn't stop there. In 2007, he co-founded Causes on Facebook, a platform aiming to promote activism and philanthropy. Later, in 2011, he launched Airtime, a live video website which, despite much fanfare, struggled to gain traction.

Beyond startups, Parker's interests branched out to other areas. He became a prominent investor, pouring money into a slew of successful companies, including Spotify, where he played a key role in its U.S. launch. His belief in the transformative power of music, evident from his Napster days, was still very much alive.

Furthermore, Parker's philanthropic efforts are worth noting. In recent years, he's focused on health and science, committing significant resources to immunotherapy research, aiming to fight cancer, and establishing the Parker Institute for Cancer Immunotherapy.

Throughout his career, Sean Parker has embodied the archetype of the Silicon Valley entrepreneur: brilliant, controversial, and always ahead of the curve. From Napster's rebellious beginnings to the hallowed halls of Facebook and beyond, Parker's impact on the tech landscape is undeniable. He remains a figure of fascination, an emblem of the relentless spirit and transformative potential of innovation.

Real Player - the start of streaming some would say

IN THE DIGITAL ANNALS of internet history, the evolution of streaming remains one of the most riveting tales. At the forefront of this transformative journey was an application many will remember: RealPlayer. In an era dominated by slow internet connections and rudimentary digital media tools, RealPlayer emerged as a beacon of progress, hinting at the future of online content consumption.

RealPlayer's story began in 1995, the brainchild of Rob Glaser, a former Microsoft executive. Glaser, driven by a vision of the internet as a platform for media distribution, founded RealNetworks and soon released the first version of RealAudio. This was a groundbreaking moment. For the first time, users could listen to audio streaming over the internet without waiting for a complete download – a novelty that seems trivial today but was revolutionary at the time.

Buoyed by the success of RealAudio, RealNetworks quickly expanded its software suite to include RealVideo. The combined capabilities of audio and video streaming gave birth to RealPlayer, a tool that, for many, was their first encounter with multimedia on the web.

The late 90s saw an explosive growth in internet users, and RealPlayer capitalized on this momentum. Its logo, a familiar sight on many web pages, signified the presence of embedded multimedia content. For users, this was a ticket to a world previously constrained by the limits of television and radio broadcasts. Live events, music, and news from around the globe were suddenly accessible from the comfort of one's home.

But success is often a double-edged sword. As RealPlayer's user base swelled, criticisms arose. Users began to grumble about its frequent updates, perceived bloatware, and aggressive marketing tactics, which bundled other RealNetwork products with the player's installation.

However, it's worth noting that RealPlayer's pioneering efforts played a pivotal role in shaping the online multimedia landscape. They demonstrated the viability and demand for streamed content, planting the seeds for the streaming giants of today like YouTube, Netflix, and Spotify.

Competition soon heated up. With the advent of Windows Media Player, QuickTime, and the explosive growth of Flash, RealPlayer found itself in a fierce battle for dominance. And while its star might have dimmed in the 2000s with the rise of these competitors, its legacy remains intact.

Reflecting on RealPlayer's journey offers a broader understanding of the digital evolution. It's a tale of innovation, of grasping the pulse of a nascent internet culture, and riding its first waves. And while newer platforms have overshadowed it, for a generation of early internet users, RealPlayer will always be remembered as the trailblazer that made online multimedia a tangible reality.

The narrative of RealPlayer paints a vivid picture of technological ambition, illustrating the meteoric rise and gradual challenges of an early digital titan in the constantly shifting sands of the tech world.

In the blossoming days of the internet, when dial-up tones were a ubiquitous soundtrack and streaming was still a nascent concept, RealPlayer emerged as a beacon. It was among the first to confront and streamline the challenge of streaming media over the internet. Gone were the days when one had to tediously wait for an entire audio or video file to download; RealPlayer opened up a world where media played as it loaded.

It wasn't long before the software became a household name. The iconic "RealPlayer" logo began gracing countless websites, signaling the dawn of an era where rich media content was just a click away. Users worldwide reveled in the newfound convenience. Features like

WEB 1.0 DOTCOM ERA DEFINED 73

"TurboPlay" significantly diminished the infamous buffering times, and the added capability of live broadcasting was nothing short of groundbreaking. RealNetworks, the power behind the player, didn't stop there. They further broadened their horizons with RealJukebox, presenting an early iteration of what would later become platforms akin to iTunes.

Yet, as with many tales of early success in the tech domain, the ascent was accompanied by challenges that tested RealPlayer's mettle. The software, in its ambition to monetize and expand its feature set, started becoming synonymous with bloatware. Users often lamented its resource-heavy nature and the inclusion of features that seemed more intrusive than helpful.

The saga of its installation process further intensified this sentiment. RealPlayer, in its various updates, had a propensity to bundle other RealNetworks products and services as default. This strategy was perceived by many as aggressive, even deceptive, leaving users cautious about even initiating an update.

Amidst this, technological vulnerabilities added fuel to the fire. As with many software solutions of the era, certain RealPlayer versions became notorious for their security loopholes. The implications weren't just functional; they were reputational.

The competitive landscape of the tech world waits for no one, and RealPlayer was no exception. As Microsoft's Windows Media Player became a staple for many, seamlessly integrated into the widely used Windows OS, and Apple's QuickTime capitalized on the iPod's staggering success, RealPlayer's dominance started to wane. The almost ubiquitous adoption of Adobe Flash for video embedding on web pages further eroded the territory once held by RealPlayer.

RealNetworks, sensing the shifting winds, attempted to rejuvenate RealPlayer, to adapt it to the emerging digital zeitgeist. There were efforts to foray into the burgeoning social media realm with features allowing video sharing on platforms like Facebook and Twitter. But these endeavors, while commendable, couldn't truly rekindle RealPlayer's former glory.

In reflecting upon RealPlayer's journey, it offers profound insights into the tech industry's cyclical nature. Pioneers can lead and shape the landscape, but maintaining that lead requires an unyielding commitment to evolution and a keen ear to the ground. While RealPlayer might not hold the digital crown today, its legacy in the annals of internet history is undeniable, a testament to a time when it reigned supreme in the world of online streaming.

The day the NASDAQ crashed

MONTHS BEFORE THE NASDAQ crash, the friendsunited mate, Kevin Doyle sold out his company to a Commerce One competitor in the UK. He sold pretty much all his stock when the price qas moving up. People thought he was crazy, as "its going to get higher". As my other good friend Ricahrd Sahonta says, "What goes up must come down" and how right that is.

The Dotcom Bubble Burst: A Digital Tumult

IN THE LATE 1990S, a euphoria swept across Silicon Valley and Wall Street alike. The internet, a relatively new frontier, was a land of opportunity and promise. Entrepreneurs, seasoned businesspeople, and investors believed that they were on the cusp of a new era of commerce, technology, and interaction. Millions of dollars poured into startups, many of which had yet to produce a cent in revenue, let alone profits. Such was the allure of the dotcom dream.

The rise was meteoric. From 1995 to 2000, the tech-heavy NASDAQ index grew over fivefold. Startups with ".com" in their names were attracting investments with just a business plan, often scribbled on the back of a napkin. Initial Public Offerings (IPOs) became legendary, with companies seeing their stock prices double, triple, or even quadruple in a single day. Paper millionaires were minted overnight. Every new venture was touted as the next big thing, and many believed the old rules of business no longer applied.

Yet, like all great gold rushes in history, the digital gold rush couldn't last forever. Beneath the surface, many of these dotcoms burned cash faster than they could raise it. Business models were often shaky at best, with profitability a distant, if not elusive, goal. The notion was to gain market share and mindshare, with profits to come "later." In many boardrooms and strategy sessions, the emphasis was on "eyeballs" or user counts, rather than sustainable revenue streams.

By the turn of the millennium, the writing was on the wall. It began with whispers and murmurs among financial analysts and skeptics. Several high-profile dotcoms reported disappointing earnings. Others revised their financial forecasts downward, with some admitting they were months, if not weeks, away from running out of cash. The market, once so buoyant and forgiving, became jittery.

In March 2000, the first major tremors were felt. The NASDAQ began a decline that would see it lose over 75% of its value by October 2002. Panic selling ensued as investors scrambled to offload tech stocks. Venture capitalists tightened their purse strings, and funding rounds that were once oversubscribed now went begging.

As capital became scarce, dotcoms folded by the hundreds. Layoffs became the order of the day. Iconic firms, once the darlings of Wall Street, went bankrupt. Others were snapped up for a fraction of their peak valuations. Startups that had lavish launch parties mere months ago now held somber goodbye gatherings.

The fallout extended beyond the dotcoms. Traditional businesses that had heavily invested in digital ventures or transformed themselves to jump on the dotcom bandwagon also felt the pain. Pension funds, once bloated with paper gains from tech stocks, saw significant erosion in their asset values.

However, in the midst of the chaos and despair, a few firms managed to navigate these troubled waters. Companies like Amazon, eBay, and Google (which went public in 2004) not only survived the bubble burst but eventually thrived. They became the new vanguards of the internet era, having learned hard lessons from the failures around them.

The dotcom bubble and its subsequent burst offer profound lessons. While the allure of new technologies and paradigms can be intoxicating, the foundational principles of business – sustainability, profitability, and value creation – remain as relevant as ever. The burst served as a sobering reminder, tempering the wild optimism of the 1990s and paving the way for a more mature and grounded digital economy in the 21st century.

The leading factors were

> Overvaluation and Speculation: Many companies during the dotcom era had stock prices that were significantly inflated, bearing little relation to their earnings or potential for profitability. Investors, driven by the fear of missing out, were buying stocks at high prices with the hope of selling them at even higher prices.
>
> Unsustainable Business Models: Numerous dotcoms lacked a clear path to profitability. They were more focused on gaining market share and "eyeballs" than creating sustainable revenue streams. When the emphasis shifted back to profitability and sound business models, many companies couldn't deliver.
>
> IPO Glut: The late 1990s saw a surge in Initial Public Offerings (IPOs). Many companies went public not because they were ready, but because it was the trend. This led to an oversupply of tech stocks, and when investor sentiment turned, there was a rush to the exits.
>
> Venture Capital Ease: Venture capitalists poured money into startups with little due diligence. As the market started to turn, this funding began to dry up, leading to a cash crunch for many companies.

Tightening of Monetary Policy: The Federal Reserve, worried about an overheating economy, began to raise interest rates in the late 1990s. Higher interest rates made borrowing more expensive, impacting both consumers and businesses.

Market Psychology and Panic Selling: As stocks began to drop, panic set in. Investors, many of whom were new to the stock market, began to sell en masse, further exacerbating the decline.

Broadband Internet Growth: Ironically, the growth of broadband exposed the limitations of many dotcoms. As consumers gained access to faster internet, they became more discerning, leading to a shakeout in the market.

Accounting Scandals: While more associated with the early 2000s (think Enron and WorldCom), accounting scandals played a role in eroding trust in the market.

Traditional Companies Entering the Digital Space: Established companies began launching their own online ventures, bringing brand recognition and deeper pockets. This increased competition for dotcom startups.

Global Economic Factors: A slowing global economy and other economic challenges in regions outside the U.S. also played a role in diminishing investor sentiment.

The U.S. Economy in the 1990s: A Decade of Dynamism

THE 1990S WAS A TRANSFORMATIVE decade for the United States. In economic terms, it witnessed an exhilarating mix of growth, innovation, and change, underpinned by a unique blend of factors that seemed to propel America to new heights.

The decade began on the heels of the late 1980s' recession, but what followed was one of the longest periods of economic expansion in U.S. history. Between March 1991 and March 2001, the American economy grew continuously, marking a decade-long boom. This period of prosperity was buoyed by various factors, both domestic and international.

A central theme of the 1990s was technological advancement. The rise of the internet and the birth of the dotcom era revolutionized industries and consumer behavior. Silicon Valley became a global epicenter for tech innovation, and startups like Amazon, Google, and eBay were born. The tech boom created new jobs, new wealth, and a surging stock market, with the NASDAQ, heavily laden with tech stocks, experiencing unprecedented growth.

Accompanying the technological revolution was financial deregulation. Measures like the Gramm-Leach-Bliley Act broke down barriers between commercial banks, investment banks, and insurance companies, setting the stage for a more aggressive and interconnected financial landscape.

But it wasn't all about tech and finance. Trade dynamics played a significant role too. The North American Free Trade Agreement (NAFTA) was signed in 1994, creating one of the world's largest free-trade zones. This agreement boosted trade between the U.S.,

Canada, and Mexico, driving economic benefits but also igniting debates about job losses in certain sectors.

On the global stage, the U.S. was unrivaled. The dissolution of the Soviet Union in 1991 marked the end of the Cold War, positioning America as the world's sole superpower. This geopolitical shift had profound economic implications. With the spread of capitalism to previously closed markets, American companies found new frontiers and consumers.

Inflation remained relatively tame throughout the decade, thanks in part to Federal Reserve policies. Alan Greenspan, the Fed Chairman, was a prominent figure, navigating the U.S. through financial hiccups like the 1997 Asian financial crisis. His management and occasional interventions earned him the moniker "Maestro."

Of course, the decade was not without challenges. Income inequality began to widen, a trend that has persisted into the 21st century. And as the decade drew to a close, warning signs flashed. The irrational exuberance, as Greenspan once termed it, around tech stocks led to the dotcom bubble, which began to burst in 2000, foreshadowing the tumultuous early 2000s.

Reflecting on the 1990s, it's a tapestry of dynamic change, marked by unprecedented growth, technological marvels, and shifting global paradigms. It was a decade when America, bolstered by economic might and innovation, stepped confidently into the new millennium, even as shadows of future challenges began to emerge.

The Dotcom Delirium: A Dive into Overvaluation

THE LATE 1990S WAS a time of heady optimism and frenzied excitement in the world of finance and technology. As the internet emerged from its infancy, venture capitalists, amateur investors, and entrepreneurs alike were entranced by its promise. Dotcom companies, so named for the ".com" in their web addresses, sprouted up like mushrooms after a spring rain, each proclaiming to be the next big thing. But amidst this explosive growth lay a volatile undercurrent: the severe overvaluation of these dotcom entities.

At the heart of the dotcom boom was a profound belief in the transformative power of the internet. Traditional metrics of company valuation, such as earnings, profitability, or even revenue in some cases, were cast aside. Instead, factors like website visitors, page views, and other nebulous metrics became the new gold standard. Companies that hadn't made a dime in profit were securing million-dollar investment deals. Initial Public Offerings (IPOs) became events of spectacle, with stocks often doubling or tripling in value on the first day of trading, driven by a frenzy of investor demand.

The narrative of the era was one of disruption. It was widely believed that these new dotcoms would reshape industries, rendering traditional brick-and-mortar businesses obsolete. This belief system led to an environment where anything seemed possible. Startups with little more than an idea sketched on a napkin were securing massive valuations. The phrase "Get big fast" became the mantra, as companies prioritized growth and market share over profitability, assuming that profits would naturally follow.

There's no denying that some of these valuations were built on genuine innovations and sound business models. But many were based on shaky premises, or worse, no real business plan at all. The speculative nature of these investments became evident in stories of retirees pouring their life savings into dotcom stocks, or taxi drivers giving stock tips.

But like Icarus flying too close to the sun, the high-flying dotcoms began to feel the heat. By the early 2000s, it became clear that many of these companies were burning through cash at unsustainable rates. The promise of future profitability began to wane, and as it did, investor sentiment shifted. The bubble that had inflated so rapidly began to burst, leading to a massive sell-off in dotcom stocks.

In retrospect, the overvaluation of the dotcom era is often attributed to a mix of unchecked optimism, a lack of understanding of the nascent internet business models, and the herd mentality of investors. Lessons were undoubtedly learned, with the pain of the dotcom crash still fresh in the minds of many. Yet, the era also laid the foundation for genuine tech giants and innovations that have since transformed the global economy.

The Interest Rate Rollercoaster: Navigating the Dotcom Era

THE LATE 1990S PAINTED a picture of a U.S. economy that was both vibrant and burgeoning. Technological advancements promised a new digital frontier, and investors, spurred on by tales of overnight millionaires, raced to stake their claims in the world of dotcoms. At the heart of this fervor lay a seemingly innocuous factor: interest rates. The role they played in both the ascent and descent of the dotcom bubble offers an insightful lens into the intricate dance between monetary policy and investor behavior.

In the initial years leading to the dotcom boom, the economic landscape of the U.S. was characterized by powerful growth, enviable employment figures, and inflation that remained surprisingly tame. The Federal Reserve, seeing no immediate red flags, maintained low interest rates. This choice, while seemingly benign, had profound implications. Cheap capital became the order of the day. Startups found themselves awash with funding options, and investors, eager for higher yields than what traditional avenues like bonds could offer, poured their wealth into the stock market. Tech stocks, with their allure of groundbreaking innovation and unmatched returns, became the darlings of Wall Street.

Venture capitalists weren't immune to this allure. With an abundance of low-cost capital at their disposal, they embarked on what can only be described as a dotcom shopping spree. The strategy was simple yet audacious: fund a multitude of startups, knowing very well that while many would flounder, a select few might emerge as goldmines. The dotcom landscape, fueled by this influx of easy money, expanded at an unprecedented rate.

However, as the 90s progressed, this sunny narrative began showing its first cracks. The Federal Reserve, under the watchful eyes of Chairman Alan Greenspan, detected whispers of an economy that was perhaps running too hot, too fast. Traditional metrics might not have screamed 'inflation,' but the Federal Reserve wasn't taking chances. Between June 1999 and May 2000, it decided to increase interest rates multiple times, intending to introduce a semblance of calm in what was becoming an overheated economic environment.

The ramifications of these hikes were swift and stark. Dotcoms, many of which were no strangers to operating losses, found the once-plentiful funding streams drying up. The cost of borrowing surged, and as it did, a newfound skepticism crept into the investment community. Tech stocks, once seen as the golden ticket to unparalleled wealth, were now being viewed with a more discerning eye. Bonds, with their promise of stability and now enhanced returns thanks to the interest rate hikes, began luring investors back. The tech-heavy NASDAQ, sensing this shift in sentiment, responded with a downward spiral.

This changing landscape was further complicated by a series of corporate scandals and companies that failed to deliver on their lofty promises. The optimism of the early dotcom days turned to caution, which soon gave way to an all-encompassing fear. Investors, sensing the tide turning, raced to sell off their holdings. The once mighty dotcom bubble, stretched thin by overvaluation and unfettered speculation, finally burst.

Skepticism and the Dotcom Bubble: Doubt's Double-Edged Sword

THE DOTCOM ERA WAS a time of unmatched optimism. Entrepreneurs, investors, and even everyday individuals believed that we were on the cusp of a new digital frontier where traditional rules of business might no longer apply. It was an age of "new paradigms" and "endless growth." However, as with any period of intense exuberance, there existed an undercurrent of skepticism. And as the bubble expanded, this skepticism played an increasingly significant role in its eventual unraveling.

In the earliest days of the Dotcom boom, skepticism was often sidelined. Stories of startups with no profits (and sometimes, no clear business models) achieving sky-high valuations were celebrated, not scrutinized. The promise of the internet seemed limitless, and naysayers were often branded as out of touch or unable to grasp the impending digital revolution.

However, as the late '90s rolled on, a few discerning voices began to rise above the cacophony. Financial analysts and seasoned investors started questioning the valuations of companies that, in many cases, had never turned a profit. They wondered about the sustainability of businesses that burned through cash at alarming rates, buoyed only by successive rounds of funding and the promise of future profits.

The media, always with a finger on the pulse of popular sentiment, began to pick up on this skepticism. Stories of failed dotcoms, once relegated to the back pages, began to feature more prominently. Profiles of overnight millionaires were gradually replaced by tales of layoffs, bankruptcy filings, and shattered dreams.

And then there was the general public. Initially enamored by the promises of the dotcom world, many began to feel the pinch as companies they'd invested their savings in started to falter. This personal experience with loss only fueled their skepticism, leading to a more cautious approach to tech investments.

The skepticism reached a crescendo when the broader economic indicators, coupled with rising interest rates, hinted at an economy that was not as robust as once believed. The stories of unfathomable success were now juxtaposed with tales of spectacular failures.

When the bubble burst, many pointed fingers at overeager investors, unscrupulous entrepreneurs, or even the media for overhyping the dotcom promise. However, it's essential to recognize the role skepticism played in this narrative. In many ways, skepticism acted as a counterbalance, a necessary corrective force to unchecked optimism. It prompted questioning, encouraged due diligence, and reintroduced a level of prudence into the investment world.

Yet, skepticism's double-edged nature meant that while it initially acted as a guard against unfettered exuberance, its intensification also accelerated the bubble's collapse. As doubt spread, it sparked panic selling, leading to a self-fulfilling prophecy of plummeting tech stocks.

Survivors and their Strategies

Google: A Journey from Dorm Room to Digital Dominance

IN THE HEART OF CALIFORNIA'S Silicon Valley, amidst a frenzied Dotcom boom where startups rose and fell with alarming regularity, a quiet revolution was taking shape. In 1996, the World Wide Web was still in its infancy, with the notion of online search being a challenge that many sought to tackle. Amidst this backdrop, two young Ph.D. students at Stanford University embarked on a project that would, unbeknownst to them, change the face of the internet forever.

Larry Page and Sergey Brin, both in their early twenties, were not initially close friends. However, their shared passion for data and its potential to reshape the world brought them together. They began collaborating on a research project to explore the structure of the World Wide Web. Their fundamental insight was to consider the internet not just as a vast collection of webpages but as a complex network of interconnected entities. Rather than simply indexing content, they believed the relationships between pages could provide valuable insights into their relevance.

This concept led to the development of the PageRank algorithm, named after Larry Page. Instead of merely counting keyword occurrences on a page, PageRank evaluated the quality and quantity of links to a page, under the theory that valuable or trustworthy pages are more likely to be linked by others. This was a radically different approach from what other search engines were doing at the time.

As their algorithm refined and results improved, what started as a university project named "BackRub" soon began to gain attention. Recognizing its potential, Page and Brin decided to rename their project "Google," a play on the term "googol," representing the number 1 followed by 100 zeros. The name was symbolic of their mission to organize the vast amount of information available on the web.

By 1998, the duo decided to take a leap of faith. With a check for $100,000 from Sun Microsystems' co-founder, Andy Bechtolsheim, they officially incorporated Google, Inc. and set up their first office in a garage in Menlo Park, California. The modest space, which they rented from a friend, would be the birthplace of a giant. It was a classic Silicon Valley startup story.

In its early days, Google's simplistic design stood out. A clean white homepage with a logo and a search bar—a stark contrast to the cluttered, ad-filled pages of other search engines. Users quickly noticed that Google wasn't just aesthetically different; it was technically superior. Searches were faster, and results were more relevant.

Word of mouth about this new search engine spread like wildfire. By the end of the year, PC Magazine listed Google as one of the top search engines, noting its uncanny ability to return relevant results. As the new millennium dawned, Google's growth was nothing short of meteoric. Venture capital flowed in, and the company expanded rapidly, but always with an eye on its core mission: to organize the world's information and make it universally accessible and useful.

Looking back, Google's origins in a university dorm room underscore the transformative power of a great idea combined with the courage to pursue it. Page and Brin didn't set out to create a global behemoth; they merely sought a better way to search the web. In doing so, they laid the foundation for a company that would go on to redefine not just search, but the very nature of our digital lives.

Apple's Survival through the Dotcom Boom

and Bust

AS THE 1990S DREW TO a close, the shimmering mirage of the Dotcom era began to dissipate, revealing a landscape littered with the remnants of overvalued tech companies. While many iconic startups of the age met untimely demises, Apple, a company with roots predating the Dotcom boom, managed to navigate these treacherous waters and emerge even stronger.

To understand Apple's resilience, one must first journey back to its precarious position in the mid-90s. The company, once the darling of the personal computing world, was on the brink of irrelevance. Sales were declining, there was a lack of innovative products, and the Windows-Intel alliance dominated the market. The colorful iMac, introduced in 1998, was a breath of fresh air, yet Apple needed more than just a single successful product to solidify its standing in the changing tech landscape.

The true turning point came with the return of Steve Jobs. Pushed out in 1985 after internal disputes, Jobs made his comeback in 1997, bringing with him a renewed sense of purpose and vision. Jobs immediately initiated changes: trimming the product line, focusing on design-centric philosophy, and instilling a culture of innovation. He also understood the importance of strategic partnerships, striking a pivotal deal with Microsoft that ensured a version of Office for Mac, a move that surprised many but was crucial for Apple's survival.

As Dotcom startups proliferated, many without a clear business model or revenue stream, Apple continued its emphasis on product innovation and user experience. Jobs and his team saw beyond the immediate allure of the internet age. They envisioned a digital lifestyle where computers were just a part of a broader ecosystem.

Then came the iPod in 2001. While the Dotcom bubble had burst and the tech industry was reeling from its effects, Apple introduced a product that transformed the music industry. The iPod, with its vast storage capacity and iconic click wheel, wasn't just a music player; it was a statement. Coupled with the iTunes Store, which made its debut in 2003, Apple created a synergy between hardware and software, offering a seamless experience for users. This ecosystem strategy would become a hallmark of Apple's approach in the subsequent years.

It's essential to note that Apple's survival wasn't just about product launches. The company managed to maintain a robust financial position, avoiding the pitfalls of overextension that plagued many Dotcom firms. Apple's leadership was cautious yet strategic in its investments, ensuring that the company had the resources to weather downturns.

Oracle's Ascendancy and Larry Ellison's Rivalries

IN THE DIZZYING EUPHORIA of the Dotcom boom, where many companies soared and plummeted with equal vigor, Oracle remained not just a survivor but a formidable player. Its journey, punctuated by its bold CEO Larry Ellison's flair for competition and confrontation, is an intriguing chapter in the annals of tech history.

Oracle began its saga in the late 1970s, well before the Dotcom era, focusing on relational databases. By the time the 1990s rolled around, Oracle had firmly established itself in this domain. Their database solutions, integral to large enterprises' infrastructure, provided a steady stream of revenue, even as other tech companies ebbed and flowed with the vagaries of the market.

But what truly set Oracle apart during the Dotcom era was its prescience. While many companies were entranced by the allure of the consumer internet, Oracle understood the value of enterprise software. The company made several strategic acquisitions, bolstering its product suite, and expanding into areas like customer relationship management and human resources software. This diversification insulated Oracle from the worst effects of the Dotcom crash, as businesses still needed robust backend systems, even in an economic downturn.

Now, any discourse about Oracle would be incomplete without delving into the persona of Larry Ellison. Charismatic, confident, and often confrontational, Ellison's leadership style was marked by his penchant for rivalries. He had a storied history of feuds, with Microsoft's Bill Gates being a notable example. Their spats were legendary, often playing out in public forums and interviews. Ellison criticized Windows, while Gates took jabs at Oracle's software. This wasn't just corporate rivalry; it was personal.

Ellison's competitive streak wasn't limited to Gates. He had skirmishes with the heads of other tech giants like Informix and PeopleSoft. His acquisition of PeopleSoft in 2003, after a protracted battle, was emblematic of his dogged determination to expand Oracle's footprint, even if it meant clashing with adversaries.

But Ellison's aggressiveness wasn't merely about personal or corporate dominance. It was strategic. By consistently positioning Oracle against industry titans, he ensured that the company remained in the limelight, always a part of the conversation. This visibility, combined with Oracle's solid product line, fortified the company's position in a volatile market.

Larry Ellison, the co-founder of Oracle, is indeed a character larger than life, and his journey in the tech world is peppered with various anecdotes, tales, and legends that have only amplified his reputation. Here are some of the more renowned tales about Ellison:

> Japanese Fighter Jet Incident: Ellison has a penchant for adrenaline-pumping hobbies, one of which is flying aircraft. One of the most well-documented tales is about him flying a Japanese fighter jet under the Golden Gate Bridge. While Ellison has denied this story, it's become a part of the Ellison lore.

Yacht Racing: Ellison's love for yacht racing is well known. He led a team called Oracle Team USA in the America's Cup, one of yachting's most prestigious events. His team won multiple times, but what's more interesting is the lengths Ellison went to in order to ensure victory, including investing heavily in technological advancements for his boats.

Hawaiian Island Purchase: In 2012, Ellison bought a whopping 98% of the Hawaiian island of Lanai. The purchase wasn't just for the land; Ellison had visions of transforming it into a sustainable paradise, with plans for renewable energy, electric cars, and sustainable agriculture.

Rivalry with Bill Gates: Ellison's disdain for Microsoft and Bill Gates is legendary. There's a tale about how, in the 1990s, Ellison hired a private investigation firm to sift through the garbage of a research company he believed was providing biased reports in favor of Microsoft. While this was a low point in their relationship, both leaders eventually mellowed in their views about each other.

The Malibu Homes: Ellison is known for his vast real estate portfolio. One famous story revolves around his properties in Malibu, California. He's purchased numerous homes along Carbon Beach, sometimes referred to as "Billionaire's Beach". He didn't stop at just one; he bought up multiple properties, turning him into a kind of real estate kingpin of the area.

Passion for Japanese Culture: Ellison's love for Japanese culture is well known. He built a Japanese-style mansion in California that's said to have taken nine years to complete.

The estate features a man-made 2.3-acre lake, tea house, bath house, and koi pond.

CEO Return: Ellison stepped down as Oracle's CEO in 2014 but returned in 2016. His brief hiatus and subsequent return drew parallels with Apple's Steve Jobs, who also had a notable departure and return to his company.

Y2K: The Apocalyptic Bug that Wasn't

AS THE 1990S DREW TO a close, a digital Armageddon loomed on the horizon. Computer systems across the world braced themselves for the chaos that was expected to accompany the dawn of January 1, 2000. Like a plot from a bad sci-fi movie, the Y2K bug threatened to send us hurtling back into the Dark Ages. But when the clock struck midnight, the new millennium ushered in...well, not a lot, actually.

So why all the fuss? The Y2K bug was a programming error that had its roots in the dawn of the computing era. To save space on punch cards—yes, punch cards—programmers had left off the first two digits of the year in dates. So "1999" became "99," "2000" became "00," and so forth. This space-saving technique was the digital equivalent of trimming your shoelaces because you didn't like how they flopped around—a solution that made sense in the moment but would come back to haunt you later when you're tripping all over yourself.

Fast forward to the late '90s, and everyone started realizing that this oversight would soon cause a massive issue. The fear was that computer systems would interpret "00" as "1900," leading to cataclysmic failures in everything from banking systems to air traffic control. If the doomsayers were to be believed, on January 1, 2000, planes would fall out of the sky, bank accounts would revert to zero, and your Tamagotchi would turn into a gremlin.

We're talking mass hysteria, a global freak-out. Companies spent billions of dollars in what was basically the largest IT project ever undertaken. Consultants became Y2K specialists overnight, offering their services to frightened corporations at astronomical rates. They were like digital exorcists, ridding companies of this millennium demon that threatened to possess their databases.

The media, of course, had a field day. If you were a news network in 1999, Y2K was your golden ticket. The bug made its way into late-night comedy sketches and was the inspiration for numerous Hollywood doomsday scenarios. People started hoarding canned goods, water, and—as far as I can tell—a disproportionate amount of toilet paper. Even the survivalists who'd been preaching the end of days for years were like, "See, we told you so!"

And then, New Year's Eve arrived. The world held its collective breath. Midnight ticked closer, and people braced themselves for the crash of a lifetime.

Only, it didn't happen.

Instead, we all woke up slightly hungover on January 1, slightly disappointed that we didn't get to live out our post-apocalyptic fantasies. Apart from a few minor glitches here and there, the world continued spinning as usual.

It was as if humanity had studied for an exam that got canceled. Sure, we were relieved, but also a bit let down. All those canned beans for nothing!

In retrospect, the Y2K bug serves as a hilarious example of a self-inflicted wound. A problem we created, then panicked about, then solved—at great expense. In many ways, it captured the ethos of the Dotcom era: the hype, the fear, the irrational behavior, and the subsequent letdown.

So you might ask, who invented the Y2K bug?

The Y2K bug wasn't so much "invented" as it was a byproduct of early programming practices. The issue originated because programmers, in an attempt to save valuable memory space in an era when computer storage was extremely limited, commonly used two digits to represent the year instead of four. This was a reasonable solution at the time but led to the problem where systems would potentially interpret the year "00" as "1900" instead of "2000."

However, credit for raising awareness about the Y2K issue goes to a number of people. One of the early figures to highlight the problem was Peter de Jager, a computer consultant from Canada. He wrote an article in 1993 titled "Doomsday 2000" that discussed the impending problem, though he was initially met with skepticism. De Jager subsequently went on to become a well-known Y2K spokesman.

There was also Ed Yourdon, an American software engineer, who wrote the book "Time Bomb 2000," further raising awareness about the issue and advising on how to handle it. Many other computer scientists, consultants, and journalists also contributed to the growing awareness and understanding of the Y2K issue, turning it into a mainstream concern.

Reality Distortion: The Most Outlandish Predictions of the Dotcom Era

THE DOTCOM ERA—A TIME when imagination ran rampant, optimism soared sky-high, and reality? Well, reality was a mere formality, wasn't it? The Silicon Valley was buzzing like a beehive, but instead of honey, it was producing jaw-dropping predictions that even Nostradamus would have scratched his head at. Some of these projections were so outrageously off-the-mark that they've earned their own honorary wing in the Museum of Absurdity (if it existed).

Let's start with the Kozmo.com fiasco, shall we? They promised one-hour delivery of practically anything—DVDs, coffee, you name it. The only thing they didn't deliver was profitability. But back in the day, their CEO seemed convinced that Kozmo would revolutionize retail forever. Reality check? Kozmo is now just a footnote in a business school case study on how not to scale a business.

And who could forget Webvan, with their audacious plan to replace grocery stores? "Physical stores are so last millennium," they proclaimed. "Soon everyone will shop for groceries online!" Well, we all know how that turned out. Bankruptcy in just 18 months post-IPO. But give them credit for audacity; they once ordered a thousand trucks for deliveries they would never make. A thousand! Was someone planning to ship elephants?

Then there were the infamous predictions surrounding Pets.com. Yes, that sock puppet dog from their ad campaigns had the whole country believing that Fido and Whiskers would soon demand their kibble be delivered by online order only. The Pets.com executive team, in a peak moment of unrestrained enthusiasm, even declared they'd become "the Amazon of pet supplies." Well, woof-woof, guess what?

They went from IPO to liquidation faster than a greyhound chasing a mechanical rabbit. Amazon is still Amazon, and Pets.com is, alas, pushing up daisies (or perhaps, more fittingly, buried in the litter box of history).

Oh, and let's not ignore the outrageous valuations. Every founder, every venture capitalist, every amateur day-trader was convinced they were sitting on a virtual gold mine. Remember Kibu.com? No? Well, they managed to raise $22 million for a website aimed at teenage girls, only to close shop within two months of launching. $22 million! One can only assume their business plan involved capturing unicorns or discovering Atlantis.

Perhaps the most amusing of them all was the absolute conviction that the traditional brick-and-mortar companies would simply roll over and die. "Malls? What are those?" they sneered, sipping on their frothy mochaccinos, "In the future, even your grandma will buy her knitting supplies online!" Fast forward two decades, and while e-commerce is thriving, those malls are still around, aren't they? Perhaps not as bustling as before, but they've survived like the cockroaches after a nuclear explosion—irradiated, maybe, but resilient.

Then there were the grandiose visions of "the internet fridge." Remember that one? According to tech prophets, we were all supposed to have smart fridges that could order groceries for us, maybe even cook us a three-course dinner (or at least that's how it felt). Over two decades later, while we do have fridges with some online functionalities, they're far from becoming our personal kitchen assistants. I mean, has your fridge ordered milk for you lately? Didn't think so.

Another humdinger was the idea of "Internet as a basic human right," a notion still hotly debated. However, back in the Dotcom days, some actually prophesied that, by now, the entire globe would have free and unrestricted internet access. Yet, here we are, with internet deserts still existing in rural areas, and numerous countries actively restricting web access to their citizens. So much for the democratization of the digital world, eh?

Don't even get me started on virtual reality (VR). When the internet was young, people acted like we'd all be living in a virtual wonderland by 2015, Matrix-style, complete with simulated vacations and virtual office spaces. While VR has made significant strides and does offer some amazing experiences, our daily lives are far from being a continuous VR simulation—unless you count Zoom meetings as the peak of virtual existence.

But perhaps the most endearing prediction was the anticipated end of privacy concerns. With the dawning of a new, interconnected era, we were supposedly going to evolve into a society that had nothing to hide. Transparency would be the name of the game. Fast forward to today, and we're more guarded than ever. Entire industries have been built around VPNs, firewalls, and cybersecurity. The innocence of the early internet seems almost comical in its naïveté.

Domain Drama: Tales of Squatters, Thieves, and Million-Dollar Names

IN THE DIGITAL GOLD Rush that was the Dotcom era, there were many ways to strike it rich—or to strike out spectacularly. While some gambled their fortunes on shaky startups or pumped billions into digital pipe dreams, others took a different route entirely: the game of domain names. It was a wild frontier, replete with opportunistic squatters, digital claim-jumpers, and a slew of often incredible, sometimes hilarious stories that would rival any Wild West legend.

Let's set the stage. In the early days of the internet, domain names were the new real estate. Prime internet locations—those with common words or phrases—were not yet the guarded fortresses they are today. This led to the birth of domain "squatters," individuals who bought up these valuable addresses with the hopes of flipping them for a hefty profit.

But there was a twist in this get-rich-quick tale: trademark law. Large corporations started to realize the value of digital land when they found out that their brands, or close iterations of them, were registered by someone else. Thus, courtroom dramas unfolded. Many squatters argued they had as much right to these domains as anyone else. After all, they'd paid for them fair and square. However, courts frequently sided with the corporations, viewing these squats as acts of intellectual property theft. Though this derailed some squatters' dreams of easy wealth, others persisted, ever looking for loopholes and ripe opportunities.

Then there were the claim-jumpers. These were individuals who would register domains that had lapsed by mistake, usually belonging to existing companies or well-known public figures. They would then offer the domains back for a ransom, or, if they were a bit savvier, negotiate a "finders fee." Many considered it unethical, while others saw it as a game of digital survival of the fittest.

However, not all tales were fraught with controversy. In a different corner of the domain landscape were individuals who genuinely struck gold. Take, for instance, the story of the person who registered Business.com. The domain was purchased for a modest fee and was later sold for a whopping $7.5 million, a headline-making transaction that had would-be millionaires frothing at the mouth.

And let's not forget the curious cases—like the high school student who registered a domain name similar to a then-upcoming search engine. When the engine took off, he found himself in the position to sell the domain back for a sum that paid for his entire college education. Or consider the woman who, on a lark, registered a domain that would later become a hit television show's name. She ended up not just with a tidy profit, but also a small role in the show as part of her negotiated deal.

Yet, these incredible, almost magical instances were the exceptions, not the rule. The majority of squatters and opportunists ended up with unsellable, often laughable, domains that gathered virtual dust until they were eventually released back into the digital wild.

"Ping Pong Tables and Free Snacks: The Birth of Startup Culture"

IN THE FEVERISH, SKY'S-the-limit optimism of the Dotcom era, it wasn't just the investors and the media who were swept up in the hype—startup employees were in for the ride too. And that ride, more often than not, came equipped with ping pong tables, an endless supply of free snacks, and maybe even a slide connecting two floors of the office. Why? Because it was the birth of a new kind of workplace culture, one that promised not just employment, but also a lifestyle. But let's dig a little deeper into how this all came about.

My favorite examples are rocking up at Commerce Ones new building, the ex People Soft Campus in Pleasenton and we had hit the height of office buzz and had a couple of buildings that "we would grow into". I also remember my first day at Commerce One in Walnut Creek and feeling very over dressed. Before you knew it I was out there shopping, white Ralph Lauren shirt and chinos!

Before the Dotcom era, the corporate environment was often pictured as a place of power suits, strict hierarchy, and cubicle farms that looked like scenes straight out of "Office Space." Then came the Dotcom boom, and suddenly young entrepreneurs were in the limelight, steering away from the stiff, formal environments of old and replacing them with bean bags, lava lamps, and, yes, those ubiquitous ping pong tables.

Casual Fridays? That concept was rapidly taken to a whole new level. It became Casual Everydays, where flip-flops and t-shirts became the norm. Who had time for ties and jackets when you were on the verge of revolutionizing the world—or so everyone thought. The funny part is that dressing like Mark Zuckerberg before he even became Mark

Zuckerberg didn't actually make you as smart or successful as him. But hey, it was worth a try, right?

But the Dotcom era didn't just change the way employees dressed; it also redefined the office layout. Gone were the drab cubicles. In their place sprang up open-concept offices designed to boost collaboration and innovation. Of course, what they often boosted instead was noise levels and the ability to see directly onto your colleague's computer screen—perfect for judging their poor taste in YouTube videos or quietly envying their Minesweeper high score.

Then there were the free snacks, the emblem of a company's generosity and proof that it truly cared about its employees. Or perhaps it was a cleverly disguised tactic to keep people in the office for as long as possible? Either way, office kitchens turned into gourmet snack bars. Breakfast cereal, fresh fruit, and even catered lunches became commonplace. And let's not forget the espresso machines that fueled late-night coding sessions. It was like Mom's kitchen if Mom were a venture capitalist armed with a nutritionist and a bottomless credit card.

Beyond snacks and casual clothing, the culture also promoted a sense of playfulness. Some offices had video game corners, others had foosball tables, and some even had in-office gyms. It was as if Willy Wonka had taken over the corporate world, and every employee had found a Golden Ticket. The rationale behind all these frills was that a relaxed, happy employee was a productive one. But what often got lost in the shuffle was a sense of direction and responsibility. Turns out, endless perks and a culture of fun didn't automatically translate to a profitable business model. Who would've thought?

The irony of it all was palpable. In an era when many startups lacked a clear path to profitability—or even a tangible product in some cases—the one thing they didn't lack was a killer environment to not make money in. And when the bubble burst, these vibrant, game-filled offices turned into very chic ghost towns. Those ping pong tables? Sold for scrap or stashed in basements. The snacks? Cleared out faster than you can say "liquidation."

In the end, while the Dotcom era may have ushered in an entirely new approach to workplace culture, it also left us with some valuable lessons, many of them cautionary. The allure of a laid-back, perk-filled office environment remains strong, but the companies that survived learned to balance culture with strategy, perks with performance. Today, even as startups continue to ply their teams with snacks and recreation, there's a greater awareness that culture, however inviting, can't substitute for a viable business plan.

Lessons Learned and the Importance of Sustainable Business Models

AS THE DUST SETTLED on the aftermath of the Dotcom bubble burst, a vast landscape of digital ruins offered a sobering reflection of what had transpired. Among the ambitious ideas, rapid investments, and the sheer excitement of a digital frontier, many businesses had overlooked one fundamental principle: sustainability. The rise and fall of countless enterprises during this era underscored the importance of having a sustainable business model, and the lessons learned from this turbulent time have since become foundational teachings for the modern tech world.

It's easy to retrospectively pinpoint the blind optimism that fueled many of the dotcom era ventures. The allure of rapid growth, the promise of the internet, and the seemingly endless flow of venture capital made it tempting to prioritize growth over profitability. Companies poured money into marketing, expansion, and capturing market share, often without a clear path to monetization or an understanding of the customer's actual needs. The prevailing notion seemed to be that if you built it and gained users, profitability would inevitably follow.

But as companies burned through their cash reserves and the investor sentiment shifted, the lack of sustainable revenue models became painfully evident. Those without a concrete plan found themselves in dire straits. In contrast, businesses that had established solid revenue streams, understood their customer base, and operated with fiscal prudence managed to weather the storm.

The lessons were clear and multifaceted:

Understanding the Customer: A business model isn't just about how a company makes money. It's intrinsically tied to understanding what the customer values, what they're willing to pay for, and how they want to engage with a service or product.

Prudence Over Exuberance: While rapid growth and capturing market share are essential, they shouldn't come at the expense of fiscal responsibility. A balance between aggressive growth strategies and financial prudence is vital.

Adaptability: The digital landscape is ever-evolving, and companies must be ready to pivot their business models in response to technological advancements, market shifts, or changes in consumer behavior.

Long-Term Vision: Quick wins can be alluring, but a sustainable business model requires a long-term vision. It's about building a company that can adapt, evolve, and thrive over the years, not just in the immediate future.

The aftermath of the Dotcom bubble provided a stark reminder that while innovation and disruption are essential, they must be underpinned by a sustainable business model. The companies that emerged stronger from this period weren't necessarily the flashiest or the most talked-about. They were the ones that understood their value proposition, knew their customers, and operated with a clear, sustainable vision for the future.

Today, as we navigate the complexities of a digital age marked by rapid advancements and transformative technologies, the lessons from the Dotcom era are more relevant than ever. They serve as a guiding light, reminding us that while the tools and platforms may change, the principles of building a sustainable, customer-centric business remain constant.

The Perils of Herd Mentality During the Dotcom Era

THE LATE 1990S AND early 2000s were marked by a frenzied rush towards the digital frontier. The allure of the internet was magnetic, drawing in entrepreneurs, investors, and visionaries with promises of untold riches and a new way of life. But as the dotcom bubble expanded, it became increasingly evident that a more insidious force was at play, one that clouded judgment and often led even the most astute astray: the herd mentality.

Herd mentality, or the inclination of individuals to follow and mimic the actions of a larger group, has been a well-observed phenomenon throughout history. In the context of the dotcom boom, it manifested in various ways, driving many of the decisions that would later be regretted.

The rise of the internet was nothing short of revolutionary, presenting opportunities that were previously unthinkable. Early successes in the digital space painted a picture of boundless potential, and soon, everyone wanted a piece of the digital pie. But as more and more joined the bandwagon, the original vision of many internet startups became obscured. Rather than building on unique ideas or identifying genuine market needs, companies began to spring up that merely imitated the models of existing dotcom successes. Why innovate when one could replicate?

The investment community wasn't immune to this phenomenon either. Venture capitalists, seeing the astronomical valuations of internet companies, began to pour money into any startup with a ".com" in its name, often with scant due diligence. The thinking was straightforward: if everyone else is investing, it must be the right move.

Fear of missing out, combined with the allure of quick returns, created an investment frenzy.

This collective euphoria was further amplified by media coverage. Stories of twenty-something dotcom millionaires became common, and the narrative was clear – the internet was the future, and any involvement promised prosperity. This media-induced excitement further fueled the herd mentality, drawing even more into the dotcom vortex.

But as with all bubbles, reality eventually set in. The inherent flaws in many business models became evident. The saturation of similar companies meant that competition was fierce, often with little differentiation between services. The vast inflow of capital led to reckless spending, with lavish launch parties, extravagant advertising campaigns, and opulent offices becoming the norm. Yet, beneath this facade, many companies lacked a clear path to profitability.

When the bubble finally burst, the consequences of the herd mentality became painfully evident. Companies folded overnight, investments evaporated, and the dream of easy internet riches crumbled. In the aftermath, a period of introspection followed. How had so many been led astray?

The dotcom era offers a cautionary tale about the dangers of herd mentality. While the allure of following the crowd can be strong, especially in times of uncertainty and rapid change, it's essential to maintain a critical perspective. True innovation and lasting success come not from mimicking others but from understanding market needs, building sustainable business models, and, most importantly, thinking independently.

The forgotten heroes of the dotcom boom

ABSOLUTELY. THE DOTCOM era, with its heady mix of triumphs and tragedies, produced several notable figures whose contributions to the digital landscape have, over time, been overshadowed by the likes of the Amazons and Googles of the world. These "forgotten heroes" made pivotal advancements, took significant risks, or laid the groundwork for the many conveniences we take for granted in today's internet age. Here are a few:

> Pierre Omidyar: While not exactly "forgotten," eBay's quiet founder doesn't always get the attention he deserves. Omidyar's online auction site not only survived the dotcom bubble but thrived, proving that trust could be established between strangers online.
>
> Joel Hyatt and Al Gore: They co-founded Current TV, an attempt at user-generated content on a cable platform. While it didn't become the next big thing, it signaled the coming age of democratized content creation, which platforms like YouTube would eventually capitalize on.
>
> Sabeer Bhatia and Jack Smith: Founders of Hotmail, one of the first webmail services. They pioneered the concept of accessing your email from any web browser, and their innovation is a precursor to the likes of Gmail.
>
> Marc Andreessen: Though not forgotten by any means in the tech industry, the broader public often doesn't recognize

the massive influence Andreessen had on the early web. As a co-author of Mosaic, the first widely-used web browser, and a co-founder of Netscape, his contributions were foundational to the internet's growth.

Joshua Schachter: He founded Delicious, a social bookmarking web service for storing, sharing, and discovering web bookmarks. It was a precursor to the "tagging" functionality now common on many platforms.

Jeff Hawkins and Donna Dubinsky: Co-founders of Handspring, they were responsible for the Treo line of smartphones – predecessors to the smartphones we know today.

Brewster Kahle: Founded the Internet Archive, aiming to provide "Universal access to all knowledge." Today, it's a priceless resource, archiving swathes of the internet that would otherwise be lost.

Cliff Freeman: While not a tech founder, Freeman's advertising agency, Cliff Freeman & Partners, was responsible for the iconic "Where's the beef?" campaign and some of the most memorable dotcom commercials, capturing the spirit of the era.

Legacy of the Dotcom Era and the Dawn of Web 2.0

THE CLOSING YEARS OF the 20th century witnessed a phenomenon unlike any before. The Dotcom Era, with its exuberant optimism and dizzying highs, epitomized a digital gold rush. Entrepreneurs, investors, and everyday people ventured into the wild west of the World Wide Web, driven by dreams of digital dominance and untapped wealth. While many struck gold, others found only mirages, and as the dust settled, a new paradigm emerged, leading to the inception of Web 2.0.

Looking back, the Dotcom bubble left a profound legacy, teaching invaluable lessons about innovation, risk, and resilience. This tumultuous period highlighted the dangers of unchecked speculation, where companies with little more than a ".com" in their name could command staggering valuations. This feverish enthusiasm was, in part, due to the genuine transformative potential of the internet. However, it also illuminated the pitfalls of prioritizing rapid growth and market capture over sustainable, long-term business models.

When the bubble burst, it wasn't just financial portfolios that felt the shock. Public trust in the digital frontier was shaken, leading many to question the viability of online businesses altogether. Yet, from this period of uncertainty, the seeds of a more mature, user-centric internet were sown.

Web 2.0 marked a significant departure from its predecessor. No longer was the internet a one-way street where businesses simply pushed content to passive users. The new paradigm championed interactivity, collaboration, and user-generated content. Sites like Wikipedia, YouTube, and Facebook began to redefine our online experiences. These platforms weren't just websites; they were vibrant, ever-evolving communities where users were both consumers and creators.

This shift was more than just technological; it was cultural. The Dotcom Era had democratized access to information, but Web 2.0 democratized its creation and distribution. Blogs gave voice to those who had previously been voiceless. Social media platforms forged connections that transcended geographical boundaries, and user-generated content sites showcased the creativity of the masses.

Yet, the legacy of the Dotcom Era was also a cautionary tale, a story infused into the DNA of Web 2.0. Entrepreneurs and investors were more discerning, prioritizing monetization strategies, user engagement, and tangible value propositions. The memory of skyrocketing valuations without clear business models served as a reminder of the perils of unbridled optimism.

Web 2.0, while built on the ruins of its predecessor, was also its most profound legacy. The Dotcom crash had cleared the digital landscape of unsustainable businesses, leaving behind a fertile ground for innovation. Companies like Google, Apple, and Amazon, which had either originated during the Dotcom Era or matured through it, became the titans of this new age, leveraging lessons learned to build products and services that were not just innovative but indispensable.

Ah, the Dotcom Era. Some folks love to wax nostalgic about the spectacular crashes, the wild parties, and the overnight millionaires who turned out to be mere paupers by dawn. They revel in tales of lavish spending on frivolities and those unforgettable Super Bowl ads. But let me tell you, that's not the whole story. Not by a long shot.

The Dotcom Era, for all its drama, laid the cornerstone for the digital empire we stand on today. Beneath the over-hyped startups and absurd valuations was a raw, undying spirit of innovation. It was brash. It was audacious. But by God, it was necessary. We needed that wild optimism, that belief that anything was possible online, to push the boundaries of what the internet could become. Mistakes were made, yes. Fortunes were lost, certainly. But in the grand scheme of things, it was a small price to pay for the digital revolution it kickstarted.

Now, it's easy to mock those who were blindsided, who believed so fervently in the 'New Economy' that they couldn't see the cliff edge they were hurtling towards. But instead of ridiculing them, I'd tip my hat. Their audacity, their willingness to risk it all, paved the way for the rise of Web 2.0. Their failures became our lessons. Their missteps, our guidance.

And as we stand here, on the brink of yet another digital frontier, I can't help but feel a begrudging respect for those Dotcom pioneers. Because while the world remembers them for the bubbles that burst, I remember the foundations they laid. Foundations upon which empires like Google, Facebook, and Amazon now stand.

So, before we get too high and mighty, before we scoff at the 'silly' ideas of the past let's remember that innovation is a messy business. It's chaotic, unpredictable, and often, downright maddening. But as we venture into new digital realms, let's carry forward the audacity of the Dotcom Era, minus the naivety. Let's be grumpy, skeptical, but also open-minded. After all, today's wild idea might just be tomorrow's revolution.

Mentions/Credits

COMPANIES/PLATFORMS:

Netscape
Boo.com
Kozmo.com
Pets.com
Webvan
TheGlobe.com
Go.com
AltaVista
AskJeeves
Commerce One
Fuckedcompany.com
Valleywag
Digital Equipment Corporation (DEC)
Yahoo
Google
Napster
RealPlayer
Apple
Oracle
BVR LLC
Intelysis
Covisint (platform by Commerce One for automotive)

Venture Capital Firms:

Sequoia

Kleiner Perkins
Benchmark

Individuals:

Louis Monier (AltaVista)
Michael Burrows (AltaVista)
Dr. Michael Maulick (Webvan CEO)
Philip Kaplan (Fuckedcompany.com)
Dr. Louis Monier (AltaVista founder)
Larry Page (Google)
Sergey Brin (Google)
Steve Jobs (Apple)
Jeff Bezos (Amazon)
Mark Pincus (early internet entrepreneur, later Zynga)
Shawn Fanning (Napster)
Sean Parker (Napster, Facebook)
Rob Glaser (RealPlayer)
Larry Ellison (Oracle)
Thomas Gonzlas Junior (Commerce One)
David Murray-Hundley "The Grumpy Entrepreneur")

Al Gore, 92
Alan Greenspan, 71, 74
AltaVista, 45, 46, 95, 96
Amazon, 16, 24, 25, 26, 41, 57, 69, 71, 83, 94, 96
Andrew Weinreich, 39
Andy Bechtolsheim, 76
AOL, 11, 12, 19, 33
Apple, 8, 15, 33, 67, 77, 78, 80, 94, 95, 96
Apple II, 8
Apple Interactive Television, 33
Ask Jeeves, 46, 47
BBC micro, 8
Benchmark, 15, 56, 58, 59, 96
Bezos, 24, 25, 96
boo.com, 18
Boo.com, 95
Brewster Kahle, 92
Broadband Internet Growth, 70
Broadcast.com, 18
Bruce Leak, 32
Business.com, 85
BVR LLC, 95
California, 9, 76, 77, 80
Casual Fridays, 86
Cliff Freeman, 92
Cliff Freeman & Partners, 92
Commerce One, 8, 12, 17, 22, 48, 50, 51, 52, 54, 68, 86, 95, 96
Commodore 64, 8
Compaq, 22, 45, 46
CompuServe, 10

Covisint, 52, 53, 96
Current TV, 92
David Murray-Hundley, 96
David Warthen, 46
Delicious, 92
Department of Justice, 20
Digital Equipment Corporation, 45, 95
Dione Internet, 27, 28
Disney, 43, 44
Donna Dubinsky, 92
Doomsday 2000, 82
dotcom bubble burst, 21
Dr. Louis Monier, 45, 96
eBay, 15, 26, 27, 59, 69, 71, 92
Ed Yourdon, 82
eToys, 23
Facebook, 12, 36, 37, 38, 39, 40, 42, 63, 64, 67, 93, 94, 96
Fashionmall.com, 23
Flooz, 23
Friends Reunited, 35, 36, 37, 38
Friendster, 39, 40
FuckedCompany.com, 48, 49
Genesis, 24, 29
Go.com, 43, 44, 95
Google, 10, 12, 45, 46, 47, 56, 69, 71, 76, 77, 94, 95, 96
Gramm-Leach-Bliley Act, 71
Greg McLemore, 41
Handspring, 92
Harvard, 37
Hotmail, 92
Hummer Winblad Venture Partners, 41
Intel, 15, 33, 77

Intelysis, 95
Internet Archive, 92
Internet Explorer, 11
IPO, 10, 11, 16, 17, 18, 19, 22, 23, 25, 26, 38, 40, 42, 46, 70, 83
IPOs, 8, 41, 68, 70, 72
ITV, 38
Jack Smith, 92
Jason Porter, 36
Jeff Hawkins, 92
Jerry Yang, 15
Jim Barton, 33
Jim Clark, 10, 33
Joel Hyatt, 92
John Doerr, 16
Joshua Schachter, 92
Julie Pankhurst, 36
Kevin Doyle, 35, 68
Kibu.com, 83
Kleiner Perkins, 14, 16, 56, 57, 58, 96
Kozmo.com, 18, 83, 95
Larry Ellison's, 78
Larry Page, 76, 96
LinkedIn, 40
Marc Andreessen, 10, 33, 92
Mark Hoffman, 50
Mark Zuckerberg, 37, 63, 86
Markkula's, 15
Michael Burrows, 45, 96
Microsoft, 10, 11, 20, 22, 29, 32, 65, 67, 78, 79, 80
Mike Markkula, 15
Mike Ramsay, 33

Mozilla Firefox, 11
MySpace, 36, 37, 38, 39, 40
Napster, 60, 61, 62, 63, 64, 95, 96
NASDAQ, 68, 69, 71, 74
Naveen Jain, 20
Netscape, 10, 11, 13, 16, 19, 33, 57, 92, 95
New York, 14
North Star, 14
Oracle, 22, 78, 79, 80, 95, 96
PayPal, 27, 56
PeopleSoft, 79
Peter de Jager, 82
Pets.com, 18, 41, 42, 83, 95
Phil Goldman, 32
Philip "Pud" Kaplan, 48
Philips, 32, 33
Pierre Omidyar, 26, 92
Pixelon, 23
Pseudo.com, 23
PurchasePro, 19, 20
R.I.P. Good Times, 56
Real Player, 65
ReplayTV, 33
Reuters, 22, 24
Rob Glaser, 65, 96
Sabeer Bhatia, 92
Salon, 29, 30
San Francisco, 9, 29
SAP, 8, 22, 50, 51, 52
Securities and Exchange Commission, 20
Sequoia Capital, 14, 15, 56
Sergey Brin, 76, 96

Set-Top Boxes, 31
Shaq.com, 23
Shawn Fanning, 60, 61, 62, 96
Silicon Valley, 8, 15, 48, 56, 57, 58, 59, 60, 63, 64, 68, 71, 76, 77, 83
SixDegrees, 39, 40
Slate, 29, 30
smart card readers, 27
Sony Internet Terminal, 32
Spotify, 61, 62, 64, 65
Stephan Paternot, 42, 43
Steve Case, 33
Steve Jobs, 15, 33, 78, 80, 96
Steve Perlman, 32
Steve Wozniak, 15
Stock options, 9
TheGlobe.com, 42, 43, 95
Thomas Gonzlas Junior, 50, 96
Time Warner, 12, 19
TiVo, 33
Todd Krizelman, 42
Valleywag, 95
VCs, 8, 14, 15, 16
Walnut Creek, 9, 22, 86
Web 2.0, 93, 94
WebTV, 31, 32, 33
Webvan, 18, 83, 95, 96
World Wide Web, 10, 11, 15, 35, 76, 93
Y2K, 81, 82
Yahoo, 11, 12, 13, 15, 18, 22, 43, 46, 56, 95
YouTube, 31, 65, 87, 92, 93

About the Author

David Murray-Hundley, fondly known as "The Grumpy Entrepreneur," is a remarkably distinguished figure in the world of entrepreneurship and business. Renowned for his straight-talking, no-nonsense attitude, and an unshakeable resolve, he has created a reputation that reflects both his business acumen and his unique persona.

Born in the United Kingdom, Murray-Hundley began his career in the technology sector, where he quickly made his mark. His first venture was Commerce One, a successful tech startup that he co-founded in the late 90s. Despite its initial success, the company was a casualty of the dot com crash, which served as a pivotal learning experience for Murray-Hundley.

Read more at https://www.parioventures.com.

Milton Keynes UK
Ingram Content Group UK Ltd.
UKHW040720161023
430697UK00001B/61